D0782303

12/06
I.C.C. LIBRARY

Police Women

Police Women

Life with the Badge

Sandra K. Wells
and Betty L. Alt

Westport, Connecticut
London

Library of Congress Cataloging-in-Publication Data

Wells, Sandra, 1950–
Police women : life with the badge / Sandra K. Wells and Betty L. Alt.
p. cm.
Includes bibliographical references and index.
ISBN: 0–275–98477–X (alk. paper)
1. Policewomen—United States. 2. Policewomen—United States—History.
I. Alt, Betty Sowers. II. Title.
HV8023.W45 2005
363.2'082'0973—dc22 2005017187

British Library Cataloguing in Publication Data is available.

Library of Congress Catalog Card Number: 2005017187
ISBN: 0–275–98477–X

First published in 2005

Praeger Publishers, 88 Post Road West, Westport, CT 06881
An imprint of Greenwood Publishing Group, Inc.
www.praeger.com

Printed in the United States of America

The paper used in this book complies with the Permanent Paper Standard issued by the National Information Standards Organization (Z39.48–1984).

10 9 8 7 6 5 4 3 2 1

For police women—past, present, and future

Contents

Introduction

A number of books and studies about women in law enforcement demonstrate both the challenges and the rewards of such a career. Still, the truest picture of what really happens when women join "the biggest boy's club in America" comes from the voices of the women who have been or are there. Their struggle up the ladder to try to reach top-ranking positions in law enforcement is a fascinating tale of both success and failure, of fair play and politics.

However, *Police Women: Life with the Badge* is not a book that presents only the current problems of being a female in law enforcement. The book provides a brief historical perspective of the women who have been the pioneers in this field. For those females who contemplate entering the male, macho world of policing, *Police Women* discusses some of the advantages women bring to this profession. Also, advice is offered to women considering choosing policing as a career by the women who have surmounted many obstacles and broken through the brass ceiling to gradually make their mark in law enforcement.

Through research, which includes some of the writings of often-cited authors considered to be authorities on women and policing (such as Dorothy Moses Schulz, Peter Horne, Susan Ehrlich Martin, Kim Lonsway, and retired Chief Penny Harrington), the authors relate the history of police women from the 1800s to the present time.

The 2001 dissertation of author Sandra K. Wells and resources such as the International Association of Chiefs of Police, the National Center for Women & Policing, and the U.S. Department of Labor Women's Bureau provide both current statistics and information on the many problems facing women who choose law enforcement as a career. Included in the book are responses to questionnaires from police women throughout the nation who attended the September 2004 Rocky Mountain Women in Law Enforcement Conference in Pueblo, Colorado, or sent comments by e-mail. In addition, interviews with currently employed police women or retired officers add up-to-date information and stories regarding the challenges they faced and continue to face as colleagues in this tightly knit all-male profession. (Where possible, the real names of individuals have been provided. When this was not possible, a false name or simply "police woman" has been used. In Wells' dissertation, interviewees were listed only by rank, age, and agency size.)

Although statistics vary, according to the National Center for Women & Policing (2003), 8.1 percent of sworn law enforcement positions in small and rural police departments and 12.7 percent in large agencies are held by females. In sheriffs' departments, the number is considerably less. The National Sheriffs' Association (2002) indicates that out of 3,088 elected sheriffs, only 30 are female—less than 1 percent. The survey "Equality Denied: The Status of Women in Policing" (2001), sponsored by the National Center for Women & Policing, a division of the Feminist Majority Foundation, even registered a *decrease* in the percentage of police women from a 1999 figure of 14.3 percent.

A major problem is that most of the women in these agencies fill lower-ranking police positions and tend not to be promoted as rapidly as male officers. Margaret Moore, Director of the National Center for Women & Policing, stated in 2002 that women were virtually absent in the highest ranks, with women holding only 7.3 percent of top command positions. It is encouraging to note, however, that several major cities and counties, including Detroit, San Francisco, Anchorage, and Atlanta, recently have installed women in top positions as Chief of Police or Deputy Chief, Director of State Patrol, and Sheriff.

What may be alarming in regard to the future of women in law enforcement departments is the 2 percent decrease shown from 1999 to 2001. If women are no longer choosing policing as a career or are failing to be retained in this job arena, fewer women will be available to move into supervisory and command positions. Recruitment and retention of women must become priorities in all agencies.

The authors would like to thank the women and men who consented to be interviewed, responded to questionnaires, or presented material at the Rocky Mountain Women in Law Enforcement Conference. They add current information to already published research. Thanks are also given to the authors' families for their patience and encouragement; to the research staff at Colorado State University–Pueblo; to the authors' agent, Mary Sue Seymour; and to their editor, Suzanne Staszak-Silva.

CHAPTER 1

From Prison Matron to Police Chief: A History of Struggle

> Make [your employers] understand that you are in their service as workers, not as women.
>
> —Susan B. Anthony, *The Revolution*, October 8, 1868

For nearly two hundred years, women have been involved in the realm of law enforcement. As early as 1820, Quaker women entered penal institutions to provide religious and secular training for women inmates. Eventually, these volunteers were joined by other upper-middle-class women who wished to reform the morals of the female inmates and train them for employment, primarily as domestics in Christian homes. They were particularly concerned that these "fallen women" were supervised by men and were sexually vulnerable.[1]

Since these reformers also felt that cities had a corrupting influence on women, prisons for women were set in the countryside and staffed by females. This created a new profession for women—the paid prison matron. A few of these matrons were even permitted to become administrators of these institutions, which gave them new positions of authority and prestige.[2] Still, these women were fulfilling the traditional female role of nurturer and caregiver. Unlike men, they were not hired because workers were needed; they were hired because *women workers* were needed.

After the Civil War, concern grew over the care received by women, children, and juveniles who ended up in police custody. Many female inmates were poor; some were alcoholics; some were young girls who had run away from home. Sometimes police stations functioned as homeless shelters for both sexes, and in this setting, as in prisons, the females were vulnerable to unwanted sexual advances. Meals could be skimpy and unappetizing. Cells were unheated, and toilet facilities consisted of a bucket emptied each morning by a member of the "bucket brigade"—those individuals tasked to do this messy chore. Simply put, the jails of the time were wretched places for both men and women.

Using the prison matron as a model, post–Civil War female activists pushed for and won a role in the jails as police matrons. Not only did they fulfill custodial roles for females taken into police custody, but they soon began to take on duties today assigned to probation officers, interviewing accused women and making sentencing recommendations. By the 1890s, thirty-six cities in the United States were employing police matrons.[3]

In New York City, full-time police matrons were hired as early as 1845. However, in 1887 the Men's Prison Association opposed having matrons in each station house. At that time the city annually "detained 14,000 women prisoners and received 42,000 female lodgers for overnight shelter."[4] The men's association objected on the grounds of lack of space for a matron, on the violent state of the women in custody, and on the fear that the matrons would be unable to physically handle the women.

In the 1800s almost no employers offered pensions or death benefits if the male breadwinner died. Often women were hired as matrons to provide them with an income if they were unmarried or widows. A breakthrough came for one woman when, in 1893, Mary Owens, the widow of a Chicago policeman, was given the title and pay of a policeman, not a matron, and had the power of arrest. For thirty years Owens' duties consisted of visiting various courts throughout the city and actually assisting detectives in cases that involved women and children.[5]

By the early 1900s, a few more women were making their way into the all-male police bastion. Lola Baldwin, a former eastern social worker, was recruited by the Travelers Aid organization to protect unchaperoned young women at Oregon's Lewis and Clark exposition as it was believed that procurers would snatch them up for worldwide white-slave traffic. In 1905, Baldwin was offered $75 a month for the duration of the fair and was given arrest authority.[6] To help her provide surveillance of the fairgrounds, Baldwin recruited many volunteers from Portland women's clubs. Utilizing these women helped take some of the pressure off the police department, which otherwise would have had to provide extra police personnel.

Baldwin continued working after the exposition on sexual vice investigation involving young women (what she called her "police cases") but without pay. Finally, she pointed out to Portland's government officials that the city had the services of a diligent officer (herself) by day and night without any cost to them. She contended that her work was clear proof that the city needed the services of a police woman. It was not until February 1908, however, that the city council voted unanimous approval of a woman's police ordinance. In March, Baldwin took the civil service board's new "female detective" exam, scoring a 95 percent and securing a position in the department. Another woman, Lucy May Sargent, qualified for the job of Baldwin's assisting clerk. On the morning of April 1, forty-eight-year-old Lola Greene Baldwin took her oath of office[7] and, according to biographer Gloria E. Myers, began duty as the nation's first municipally paid police woman.[8]

In 1910, Alice Stebbins Wells joined the 350-member Los Angeles Police Department (LAPD) after presenting to the mayor and police commissioner a petition signed by more than one hundred influential citizens that requested the appointment of a police woman to undertake protective and preventive work among women and children. She was considered by some to be the first *real* police woman in the United States although she did not wear a uniform, did not carry a weapon, and in her pocketbook carried her badge—a man's badge until Police Woman's Badge Number One could be made. Just over five feet tall, Wells was depicted in newspapers as a "bony, muscular, masculine person, grasping a revolver, dressed in anything but feminine apparel, hair drawn tightly into a hard little knot at the back of the head, large unbecoming spectacles, small stiff round disfiguring hat, the whole presenting the ideal in the most repellent and unlovely guise."[9]

Instead of protecting the general public as policemen did, Wells' duty chiefly involved protecting women. She enforced laws concerning dance halls, skating rinks, penny arcades, movie theaters, and other places of recreation frequented chiefly by women and children. She also searched for missing persons and provided social service information to women.

A pioneer in the field of women as police officers, Wells often spoke in public as a guest lecturer, which in the early 1900s was considered to be "unwomanly." The public was extremely curious about her, and on lecture tours publicity was similar to that advertising a circus. In a small Pennsylvania town, the movie theater marquee read, "Mrs. Wells, First Policewoman—See Her!" Her status as a member of the police force was so unheard of that once while she was attempting to take advantage of the free transportation the city provided to police officers, a street car conductor refused to accommodate her. He accused her of stealing her husband's police badge.[10]

As Wells argued for women to be appointed to police departments, several municipalities across the country began hiring women chiefly for office duties. In 1912, the city of Denver hired Josephine A. Roche (who later would serve as Assistant Secretary of the Treasury in President Franklin Roosevelt's administration). Topeka appointed Eva L. Corning and Elizabeth Barr-Arthur in 1913; Kate O'Connor, Kathlyn Sullivan, and Kathryne Eisenhart (the "Three Kates") joined the San Francisco Police Department in 1914. A *major* event in policing for women occurred in 1914: the city of Milford, Ohio, appointed Dolly Spencer as the first female Police Chief in the United States.[11] Wells continued her lectures on the necessity of departments having police women and, in 1915, while attending the National Conference of Charities and Corrections, Wells became nationally known as she and other police women organized the International Association of Policewomen, which was active into the 1930s.[12]

While a few women like those mentioned here were moving into the male bailiwick, during the 1900s most police women were basically still social service workers. Like Baldwin and Wells, they were required to meet higher standards than men for police employment and were primarily assigned to clerical work, guard duty, vice work, and juvenile problems. Their duties consisted of those that males would not or could not do—conducting searches on female suspects, prisoners, or corpses and working as decoys for prostitution arrests. They typed, changed diapers, and baby-sat and, despite higher levels of education and broader professional orientation than male colleagues, were paid less than the male officers.

Another indication that these women were not considered to be officers is the fact that most departments did not issue them any type of uniform. A few may have done so, as an artist's conception of the New York City Police Department's (NYPD) first female members shows a very attractive young woman herding two obviously inebriated males. Perched on her head at a jaunty angle is a military-style cap, and her ankle-length suit sports two long rows of buttons, similar to those on a military uniform. What may be more accurate than the drawing is an actual 1911 photograph of an NYPD matron, which shows the woman tightly corseted, with an hourglass figure, long black skirt, and snug waist-length jacket with eighteen buttons.[13] For many women connected with police departments, it would be decades before they would be in uniforms similar to those men wore.

Still, by 1916 there were police women in twenty-one states, and the entry of the United States into World War I led to an increase in the use of police women, with twenty-five cities having at least a few women on their payrolls. For example, Dorothy Moses Schulz provides some specific information on cities across the United States and the number of police women employed, including major cities such as San Francisco (3), Chicago (36), San Diego (3), Denver (1), Seattle (5), San Antonio (2), and Pittsburgh (4).[14] It is unlikely, however, that most of these women were actually on street patrol; most would have been utilized in some form of support duties thought appropriate for female officers.

OFF THE DESK AND ON PATROL

By 1925, however, Elizabeth Munger, Secretary of the Committee on the Care and Training of Delinquent Women and Girls, was pushing for police women to be taken off their traditional desk duty and placed on patrol duty.

> The policewoman does not sit in an office and wait for a case to be reported. One of the important phases of her work is "patrol duty," which puts her into close contact with the real life of the community, and enables her to use the Arm of the Law, sometimes as a shield and sometimes as a support, in situations which, particularly for the youthful offender, portend an ultimate use of the Arm in its traditional punitive function.[15]

As women were gradually making their way into police departments as sworn officers, women were also entering police work as Sheriffs or Sheriff Deputies. Most of these women did not actively seek the position but were usually temporarily appointed to it upon the death of their Sheriff husbands. As early as 1870 the wife of Sheriff James Latty in Burlington, Iowa, took on the task of running the jail. However, Mrs. Latty's position was an unofficial one, and it is Emma Susan (Daugherty) Banister of Coleman County, Texas, who supposedly holds the honor of becoming the first "known" woman Sheriff. After her husband, Sheriff John R. Bannister, died in 1918, Emma was appointed by the Coleman County commissioners to complete his term of office. Apparently, she efficiently performed her duties as a law enforcement officer while still taking care of the domestic duties required in her home. However, when the county commissioners offered to place her name on the ballot for an upcoming election, she declined the offer and moved back to the family farm. In 1926 Mabel Chase of Kiowa County, Kansas, was apparently the first woman in the United States to be *elected* Sheriff. However, women were still being appointed to the position at much later dates. For example, Maude Murphy was appointed to serve out her husband's term when he died in 1944.[16] (Increases in women in law enforcement have occurred in different sizes in different agencies and at different times. A comparison of 1990 data for

Sheriffs' departments with data from other law enforcement agencies showed that women had the greatest representation in Sheriffs' departments, where they constituted 15.7 percent of all Deputies.)[17]

In addition to females becoming police women or Sheriffs, a few women were admitted to the state police force. In 1930, America's oldest statewide enforcement agency in Massachusetts saw Mary B. Randsell and Lotta H. Caldwell enter its ranks.[18] Bit by bit women were slowly infiltrating all the major areas of law enforcement and, like their male counterparts, were serving the public.

However, during the 1930s—the era of the Great Depression—jobs disappeared almost overnight. Men who thought they had stable employment were suddenly mobile, as thousands trudged along the highways or "rode the rails" seeking work of any kind. The Depression also caused problems for working women, as some were dismissed from their jobs so that men, especially those with families to support, could have paychecks. Women were encouraged, particularly if they were married, to stay at home and devote their energy to the care of their husbands and children.

Some *official* policies actually discriminated against married women. By 1932, Section 232 of the National Recovery Act specified that if both husband and wife were employed by the federal government, and if reductions were being made, one or the other would be dismissed. While this did not specifically state that wives were to be dismissed and husbands retained, usually the husbands were in higher-paying positions and remained on the job. A 1936 poll found that 82 percent of those responding, including three-fourths of the women polled, felt that women with employed husbands should not be working outside the home. Working wives were seen to be "selfish, greedy women who took jobs away from male bread-winners," and their wages were seen as "luxury" wages.[19]

State and local law enforcement agencies tended to follow federal guidelines, and the number of police women fell or, at best, remained relatively stagnant during the Depression years. Many times the women worked in separate women's bureaus within the police departments, and these women's bureaus tended to struggle along with one or two women, who eventually were incorporated into other units. Police women who retired were not replaced, and the preventive work they had done in juvenile delinquency and female criminality was assumed by social workers in other public agencies.[20]

However, during the Depression decade, training in social work could be of some help for women who wished to move into law enforcement, as a 1930 article entitled "Meet the Lady Cop" indicates. In Berkeley, California, the rules and regulations specified that "no woman police officer shall be appointed who is not a trained social worker . . . and [who does not have] some practical experience in work with individual delinquents."[21]

This concept of a social worker, of nurturer and caregiver, instead of someone involved in law enforcement and protection of the public was ever present. Perhaps a comment in a 1925 article entitled "Woman's Place in the Police Department" explains it best:

> In many ways the position of a woman in a police department is not unlike that of a mother in a home. Just as a mother smooths out the rough places, looks after the children and gives a timely word of warning, advice or encouragement, so the policewoman fulfills her duty. . . . [With] the welfare of children, girls and women for their field of service, policewomen have been given a task—to perform quite different from that of their fellow policemen.[22]

The article continues by citing a police woman in "a large eastern city" who resigned her position because she had been assigned to duties that involved gathering evidence. She had joined the department to "help fallen women and wayward children" instead of doing work that she felt could be better done by men.

Whether due to the lack of available jobs or to the public's continuing disdain for women in a man's profession, women had lost some ground in entering police work, and by the end of the Depression (in the early 1940s), there were only a thousand publicly funded police women hired by fewer than 3 percent of the nation's law enforcement agencies.[23] The Depression decade had taken a toll on women's progress in policing.

Then, with the advent of America's involvement in World War II, openings in police departments were created when millions of men either enlisted or were drafted for military service. Both male and female auxilliaries replaced police officers who either had volunteered or had been drafted into the armed forces. Activated through legislation that stipulated that they would be disbanded when regular officers returned from active duty, the male auxilliaries usually acted as full-time officers, performing general police duties and sometimes getting involved in violent episodes. On the other hand, the women generally did not replace men and did not carry firearms. They inspected dance halls and nightclubs, served as dispatchers or traffic control agents, and worked as school crossing guards. "Lady cops" in Detroit spent their shifts hunting for missing girls or inspecting amusement parks, theaters, and beer gardens that might be serving liquor to juveniles. The women were also utilized in cases in which young victims of sex crimes refused to talk with a male investigator. Labeled "police women" by some municipalities, these women rarely had full police powers, although they tended to be the first females to don police-style uniforms. "While the war did spawn Rosie the Riveter, there was no Connie the Crimefighter."[24]

POSTWAR POLICE WOMEN

However, writing in May 1945, at the end of the war in Europe, Irma Buwalda, a Consultant for the Federal Security Agency, stated that the future for females in policing might be getting better, as there was apparently a rising demand for police women among law enforcement executives. She cited as support the two hundred such requests received by Captain Rhoda Milliken, Chief of the Women's Bureau of the Washington, D.C., Metropolitan Police Department and Commissioner Eleanor L. Hutzel, head of the Woman's Bureau in the Detroit Police Department. A major problem would be the lack of training, as less than 3 percent of America's police units contained qualified police women at that time. Buwalda encouraged schools and universities to make women aware of the need for women in policing and to guide them toward that service field by instituting a curriculum that would encompass such subjects as delinquency and crime prevention. She also mentioned that in order to help any newly appointed police women in local communities, the National Advisory Police Committee on Social Protection of the Federal Security Agency had "sponsored the preparation of a policewomen's manual, outlining the duties of the job, recommended qualifications, how to handle cases, patrol, and community relations."[25] Buwalda was realistic enough to realize that support from the public would be needed if more police women were to be appointed but felt that postwar communities should look toward that goal.

However, it was not just the perception that police women could be an asset to a department that contributed to the gradual rise in their numbers. One of the major reasons women may have had a better chance at law enforcement positions was that when the men were discharged from military service after the war, not all of them returned to their previous jobs as policemen. The United States was converting from wartime production to peacetime activities, and employment was readily available in manufacturing and other types of organizations. The G.I. Bill made it possible for many to take advantage of a university education, and a significant number of those who received degrees were in great demand in the expanding economy and moved into positions outside law enforcement.

Therefore, many police women, including auxilliaries, were not faced with layoffs when the soldiers returned. An increase in juvenile delinquency in the postwar years provided an additional need for female personnel. However, assignments for women became more diversified; women often were partnered with men and were trained in the use of firearms and expected to carry them. They were utilized in undercover work as decoys and in plainclothes assignments instead of merely investigating morality-based crimes such as prostitution.[26]

Across the United States, steady progress for police women was being made. By 1950 there were more than 2,610 publicly employed police women in America, although this was only slightly more than 1 percent of all police. In 1960 the U.S. census listed 5,617 police women or an increase to about 2 percent of officers. In the decade from 1950 to 1960 the number of police women doubled, increasing by 3,000.[27] Yet women had little opportunity for promotion and were offered only limited job placement. According to Captain Diane Harber, who joined the LAPD in 1957, "We had two choices: go to the Youth Division or to the jail. Most of us went directly to jail."[28]

THE WINDS OF CHANGE

Nevertheless, the modern era of women in law enforcement was on the horizon when, in 1961, a lawsuit was filed against the New York City Police Department. Officer Felicia Shpritzer sued the department on behalf of all police women who had been barred from taking the promotional exam for sergeant. She won the case, and she and Gertrude Schimmel became the first two women sergeants. Of course, change did not occur overnight, but Shpritzer's win opened the supervisory ranks to competent police women throughout America.[29]

In 1965, during President Lyndon Johnson's administration, the role of the federal government in criminal justice was expanded. Johnson appointed the President's Commission on Law Enforcement and the Administration of Justice (also known as the President's Crime Commission) to analyze crime in the United States. The commission recommended that criminal justice agencies form an integrated system with better coordination among police, courts, and correctional facilities. In addition—and this was particularly important for women—it called for upgrading personnel in the system by widening women's assignments, recruiting women and people of color, raising selection standards, and providing more rigorous training to all criminal justice system personnel. It further suggested that recruiting and hiring women and minorities was necessary for the good of police-community relations.[30]

While all these recommendations looked good on paper, they resulted in only minor improvements for female police. A 1967 survey of 161 police departments in the largest American cities demonstrated that there were still only 1,792 women with actual police powers such as patrolling the streets and carrying a weapon. Typically, women made up only 1 to 2 percent of a police force, if they were present at all. Many police departments still had informal policies that discouraged the hiring of women. For example, even after the President's 1965 crime commission recommended recruiting and hiring women, the LAPD refused to hire new female officers for four years and filled vacancies with males. Ed Davis, Los Angeles Police Chief, told women that they did not belong in patrol cars and that they could not be trusted with guns "during that time of the month."[31]

Occasionally, in some police departments women were moving out from behind their desks. A 1970 article in the *Memphis Press Scimitar* appears under the headline "Women to Ride in Police Cruisers" and explains that this event is part of an experimental program. Patrol Woman Freeda Bowers was the first female officer assigned to a police cruiser, but the article states that the assignment was to be only temporary. Deputy Chief W. O. Crumby indicated that if the program was effective, a total of three women from the department's training academy would be assigned to cruisers.[32] However, as in Los Angeles, most women who worked in police departments across the country were still primarily assigned to clerical duties or social work.

The push to recruit minorities also saw more African Americans on police forces, although blacks had served on police forces since the nineteenth century. The first black police officer was appointed by a Chicago mayor in 1872; by 1894 twenty-three black officers were employed in that city.[33] While these earlier officers were males, black women slowly began to appear in departments across the nation, especially in major cities. (Martin and Jurik cite 1992 U.S. Department of Justice data that indicated that although African American women "continue to be greatly underrepresented . . . one-third of the women officers are women of color, and women make up 19% of all black officers.")[34]

Of course, being hired did not necessarily mean African American females would receive equal treatment. Generally, white women were more likely to be treated better by male officers and to be placed in more traditionally female positions within a department. As one black woman indicated, "White women were put on a pedestal, treated like wives. . . . A lot of white women got jobs doing typing for commanders. . . . They're high priced secretaries."[35]

However, after World War II, a new type of police job would be available that allowed women (white or black) minimal admittance to many agencies as America retooled its factories from manufacturing products for battle to manufacturing products for civilian life. New automobiles, which had been all but nonexistent for civilians for several years, were now becoming abundant and creating parking problems in most cities across the United States. The late 1950s and 1960s saw the emergence of women in minor positions in many police departments as "parkettes" or "meter maids." It is interesting to note that men did not fill these positions, and the women were labeled "maids." Still, it was often the only way for a female to get her toe in the door of a police agency.

These women with their frivolous titles were hired by police departments with the sole purpose of controlling parking and directing traffic. Dressed in skirts and walking or driving small motor scooters, they were familiar figures in many cities across America. Retired Deputy Police Chief Charlene Graham began her police career as a meter maid in Pueblo, Colorado, during the late 1960s. Graham recalled that she was one of five full-time and two part-time meter maids who walked their patrol areas, as motor scooters were unavailable. The police department did not have regular summer uniforms for the women. Theirs were "homemade" (made by a dressmaker) and consisted of a navy above-the-knee skort (a combination skirt-shorts garment) and gray uniform shirt. The winter uniform included the shirt, black ski pants, sweater, pea coat, and earmuffs. When asked about problems she might have encountered in her job, Graham laughed as she related one incident.

> Everyone hated to get a parking ticket. You may not believe it, but there were more disputes over a dollar parking ticket than might have occurred for something more serious. I remember one time when I was writing a ticket for overtime parking, and the man who owned the car came up just as I was tucking it under the windshield wiper. He was so angry at me that he took the ticket, tore it into little pieces right in front of me and tossed them on the ground. What he didn't realize was that a uniformed officer was parked directly across the street and watched him do this. The officer came over and gave the man another parking ticket and also a ticket for littering.[36]

It would be two and a half years before Graham would be able to give up her position as a meter maid and move into the ranks of male officers at a salary increase to $750 per month, in 1972. Still, this move was not accomplished easily. There was a separate written test for those applying to be police women. In addition, unlike male applicants, women were required to have at least two years of experience or two years of college. Graham made the grade and was soon in uniform, complete with an "issued purse," which had a special compartment for her gun—an Air Weight snub-nosed .38-caliber. "The women were issued this type of gun because a standard gun was considered to be too heavy for us to use," Graham explained.

As in Graham's case, occasionally, there were some signs in other states of a breakthrough for female officers. In Indianapolis two women suggested to their police academy instructor that they should be on patrol. The Sergeant instructor told the women that if he were ever in charge, he would allow women to become patrol officers. When he became Chief in 1968, he was reminded of his promise. As a result, Indianapolis police women Betty Blankenship and Elizabeth Coffal put on uniforms and gun belts and got into their marked police car to answer calls for service, "the first all-female radio car assignment in the history of women in policing."[37] These two abandoned the traditional role of police women as caregivers and assumed the role of crime fighters along with their male counterparts. Even so, women working the streets as police officers were rare. However, change was in the wind.

The early 1970s ushered in the modern era of women in policing. It began in 1969 with President Richard Nixon issuing Executive Order 11478, which stated that the federal government could not use gender as a qualification for hiring. Then, in November 1971, the Supreme Court ruled in *Reed v. Reed* that the equal protection clause in the Fourteenth Amendment prohibited discrimination on the basis of sex. Because of these actions, both the Executive Protective Service and the Secret Service hired female agents, and in July 1972 the FBI assigned two women to its academy for training special agents.[38] Municipal police departments could see the handwriting on the wall and realized that they, too, would have to assign women to training and police tasks identical to those of men.

In March 1972 Congress passed the Equal Employment Opportunity Act (EEOA), which applied Title VII of the 1964 Civil Rights Act. This act prohibited employment discrimination to state and local government on the basis of race, color, religion, sex, or national origin.[39] It appeared that women had won the battle for equal employment in law enforcement. At last they would be allowed to go on patrol, receive promotions, and earn the same salaries as male officers.

Also in 1972, Pennsylvania became the first state to employ women for state police duties identical to those of men. In July, fourteen female troopers graduated from the training academy and were assigned to general patrol duties throughout the state. Many other states soon followed suit, although there originally was resistance from South Carolina, New Jersey, and Alabama state police agencies.[40] (Author Betty Alt remembers a Massachusetts State Trooper speaking to her social problems class at Middlesex Community College in 1972. When some of the women in the class questioned the lack of females as troopers, the man explained that height requirements were 5′ 10″ with a weight requirement of 180 pounds. "Most women cannot meet the height requirement," he explained, "and most women will not admit that they weigh 180 pounds.")

At the same time that a few women were being admitted to state patrol agencies, the military also got on the bandwagon. In October 1977 the first class of Military Police One-Station-Unit Training (OUT) at Fort McClellan, Alabama, included females among its trainees. By 1978, the women had not only invaded this formerly all-male force, but OUT had a woman, Brigadier General Mary E. Clarke, as its new Commander.[41]

Although the EEOA had created changes in the American workforce as a whole, female police officers still faced a number of problems, including a lack of opportunities for promotion. Certain jobs, especially patrol, were looked on more favorably as potential assignments for women, but women were still usually relegated to desk work. In all types of law enforcement, women began to press for jobs within the system that would be commensurate with their years of experience and performance and that would give them a chance for job mobility.

Prior to the EEOA, women were not permitted to take the same promotional examinations as men and were denied promotion except within their own special units. During the 1970s women officers demanded their right to be allowed to test for promotions and to be placed in positions that previously had not been available to them. In response, police administrators indicated that women could, in fact, be promoted, but only in their own bureaus because most lacked the full "police experience" of patrol duty.[42] Of course, these same administrators ignored the fact that they had denied women the opportunity for patrol duty in the first place.

By 1975 most sociologists and researchers in the criminal justice field understood that not all good officers were men, even though, of the various studies conducted during the following ten years, most reached the conclusion that police women were not as capable as men. The study that was the exception to the negative studies was performed in response to a sex discrimination lawsuit filed against the Philadelphia Police Department which contended that police women did not patrol as well as policemen. The study followed one hundred men and women on patrol for two years, and the indication was that women did not project power and strength to the same degree as male officers. Also, men rated higher on building searches. However, the study indicated that women were as diligent in making arrests as their male colleagues, with no difference in the number of arrests. In addition, female police officers were rated better than male officers on handling citizens carrying guns, family disturbances, and automobile stops. The end result of the study was that women handled patrol just as safely and efficiently as men, and the federal judge overseeing the suit ordered the police agency to stop its discriminatory practices against women.[43]

A gradual increase of women in policing could be seen in the latter part of the 1970s. The figure increased in 1979 to 5.9 percent nationwide, with a figure of 6.9 percent of the police in cities with populations over 250,000.[44] Slowly the ranks of police women were growing, and in the mid-1980s had reached 7.6 percent of local police officers.[45]

HEADING TOWARD THE TWENTY-FIRST CENTURY

While the ranks of women in local, state, and federal law enforcement reached 11 percent in the 1990s, the rate of growth was slow—barely more than 3 percent from 1990 to 1998.[46] For women filling the position of Sheriff, the numbers are considerably smaller than those for police women. For example, in Georgia, of the 159 elected Sheriffs, Jacquelyn H. Barrett is the only woman. According to a report from Fulton County, Georgia, she also "holds the distinction as the first African-American female Sheriff in United States history."[47]

Women have joined sheriffs' departments at lower ranks and hold positions of Sheriff Officer or Deputy. However, according to statistics from the Department of Justice, of the 174,673 full-time sworn personnel in sheriffs' departments, only about 16 percent were women in 1997. This percentage varied slightly depending on the size of the jurisdiction, with some areas showing a larger percentage while others showed a smaller one. For example, in jurisdictions with populations of half a million to a million, the rate of females in sheriffs' departments was 20 percent; in jurisdictions with populations under 25,000, the rate dropped to 12 percent.[48]

As with female Sheriff Deputies, most of the strides women made in police departments were in metropolitan areas with large populations. A recent study by the National Center for Women and Policing indicated that Pittsburgh led the nation, with women representing 25 percent of its police force. The survey also emphasized that eight out of the ten police departments with the largest numbers of women had either followed mandatory hiring policies regarding women in the past or currently were under such policies. However, in 1991, the federal court lifted an order for the Pittsburgh Police Department to hire minorities, which appears to have taken a toll on female employment. "Since that year, females have made up only 8.2 percent of new police officers hired, a figure below the national average."[49]

Over the past thirty-five years, much of the progress women have made in obtaining employment in police departments has been attributable to court-ordered recruiting and hiring practices aimed at increasing the diversity of police forces. Still, by 1996 the U.S. Department of Justice indicated that the number of police women had risen to only 10.1 percent of all full-time sworn personnel.[50] By 1997, a study of one hundred of the largest law enforcement agencies in America revealed that women still represented only 12 percent of the police force. While this figure can be viewed as a success, there was considerable resistance to this growth, and women often had to bring litigation against departments to overcome official resistance. "Organizations that represent women police officers find this rate of growth of concern, particularly when compared to the ratio of women to men in the U.S. population."[51] (Females comprise 51 percent of the population; males, 49 percent.)

As the world settles into the twenty-first century, police women still face barriers in law enforcement. In a 1979 issue of the *Police Journal*, Peter Horne predicted that 50 percent of sworn police officers would be women by the year 2000.[52] Yet a spring 2003 report by the National Center for Women & Policing showed that prediction had not come to pass. Women comprise only 12.7 percent of all sworn law enforcement positions in large agencies, 8.1 percent in small and rural agencies, and 14.4 percent in federal agencies. "In 2000 and 2001, the representation of women in large police agencies *actually declined* from the year before—from 14.3 percent in 1999 and 13.0 percent in 2000 to 12.7 percent in 2001."[53]

In a 2004 article on the decreasing number of women in policing, Margaret Moore, Director of the National Center for Women & Policing and the highest-ranking woman ever to have served in the Bureau of Alcohol, Tobacco & Firearms emphasized the problem:

> The fact that the percentage of women in law enforcement is decreasing is alarming. Not only is there a smaller percentage of women in policing, but women are virtually absent at the highest ranks of law enforcement, holding only 7.3% of top command positions. In fact, more than half (55.9%) of large agencies surveyed report no women in top command.[54]

Moore went on to explain that widespread bias in selection policies and recruitment practices keeps the numbers of women in law enforcement artificially low. She also stressed that "on the job, women often face discrimination, harassment, intimidation, and are maliciously thwarted in their attempts to move up the ranks."[55]

For those women contemplating entering law enforcement, Moore's comments on continuing prejudice and discrimination against women must be particularly depressing. Also, from the research that has been undertaken over the past few years, it appears that Peter Horne's prediction was overly optimistic. At the present rate of growth, apparently women will not achieve equality with men in police agencies for several decades.

CHAPTER 2

Breaching the Blue Wall

> The uneasy sense of battles won, only to be fought over again, of battles that should have been won, according to all the rules, and yet are not . . . how many women feel it?
>
> —Betty Friedan, *The Second Stage*, 1981

Although policing is still one of the few remaining bastions of male dominance, in ever greater numbers women have been challenging this "blue wall." Until recently, police culture, like the military, has always been male in population and perspective. However, beginning in the 1970s an increasing number of women took up the battle to invade the hallowed male halls of this bureaucracy. Not wanted, but mandated by law to be integrated into policing, these women faced tremendous obstacles as they sought full equality.

Male officers have often been plagued in the media by the stereotype of the "dumb cop," an image that also would be applied to women. In books, movies, and television, the policeman always ignored obvious clues to a crime and jumped to the wrong conclusions regarding possible suspects. The male police detective constantly needed the help of Batman, Sherlock Holmes, Hercule Poirot, or the Thin Man to solve a crime. Like the male officer, the female officer was originally stereotyped by the media as inept and in the wrong career. Although she usually "got her man," the picture of blond, bouffant-haired Angie Dickinson chasing a suspect in her spike heels provided an unrealistic stereotype of female cops. It was not until the television series *Cagney and Lacy* aired that female officers began to be portrayed in roughly the same manner as male officers, although occasional segments in that series tended to place before the viewing audience the age-old stereotype that women might not be able to adequately perform required duties.

PERCEPTIONS OF WOMEN IN POLICING

Still, society's attitude about women in policing was slowly changing, and studies were being conducted regarding the public's overall impression of women police officers and whether they should be in that profession. Although the studies showed varying results, these earlier works (conducted in the turbulent era of the 1970s and with some differences between male and female respondents) did indicate that, in general, both male and female citizens and male officers appeared to be "wrought with misperceptions about the police role and the idea of females as patrol officers."[1] The comment of one police woman (married and with three stepchildren over the age of twenty-one) illustrates the perception that females would be too fragile or too fearful to do the job:

> I was the smallest person. . . . They [male officers] didn't feel I could do the job. They tried to get me into fighting situations to see if I would back down. They told me, "You know, if you aren't strong enough or are going to be a coward, we have to find out fast and get you out of here."[2]

As late as 1980, after a decade of integration in policing, Susan Martin found that the male officers indicated they wanted a partner who would be tough and who could fight and back them up. The perception was that females could not be counted on in instances where there might be confrontation. Ella Bully-Cummings, who would eventually become Chief of the Detroit Police Department, recalled that when she first entered that "macho, paramilitary culture" in 1977, "some of the male officers feigned illness to avoid working with her. Some on patrol with her sometimes would call for backup even before arriving at crime scenes."[3]

Even women tended not to be supportive of their sex. In his 1981 study on the occupation and introduction of female officers into policing, P. W. Remmington questioned a few female officers about whether they would prefer a male or female partner. *Every female chose a male*. A 1982 study by Vega and Silverman indicated that 48 percent of male officers interviewed felt that women should not even be considered for jobs as police officers. Bell's 1982 study indicated that citizens also believed female officers were not as good as male officers, particularly in violent situations.[4]

These attitudes continue to be prevalent among some of the population. For example, a 1999 study examined attitudes of college students at a small university in the Northeast—the primary age group of new police recruits. Conclusions from that research indicated that females in the study overwhelmingly agreed "that women had what it took to be 'good cops.'" On the other hand, while attitudes of male college students toward women as police officers showed some change from earlier studies, as might be expected, they still tended to be negative. Males especially were least supportive of police women when the situation involved the question of physical strength and whether the women could handle violent or dangerous situations.[5]

Unfortunately, the male's perception may still affect women entering the force. In response to a 2004 questionnaire (see Appendix 2), Captain Margaret T. in Virginia indicated that after working eighteen months in Personnel she felt that "even many women today don't feel they have the muscle to do the job. They still feel that strength is what you need to be a police officer." However, regardless of perceptions, when police departments were directed after 1972 to recruit females to fulfill specifications of the EEOA, police women began to appear in larger numbers in departments across the United States.

EFFECTIVENESS OF RECRUITMENT

Recruitment of women into the male-dominated police world has been slow, and some law enforcement agencies had to be pushed into recruiting women.[6] Because some police departments failed to follow (or were slow to implement) the EEOA rules and actively recruit females, lawsuits were filed and consent decrees were initiated. The consent decree was an agreement submitted in writing to a court in lieu of a lawsuit trial and, once approved by a judge, was legally binding. The decree would usually last a specified period of time, during which a department had to demonstrate substantial compliance with the provisions listed in the decree. One of the major areas that appeared in many decrees was the management and supervisory measures needed to promote civil rights integrity.[7]

Therefore, due to the consent decrees, women were made by law to be "acceptable," and agencies were expected to recruit them. This does not mean, however, that changes occurred overnight, and in many cases, unless the courts kept a watchful eye on police departments, the decrees were ignored. For example, the Pittsburgh Police Department was under a court order from 1975 to 1991 that mandated that for every white or African American male hired, one white female or African American female was to be hired. By 1990, the department showed an impressive rate of 27.2 percent female officers, the highest rate in the country. Once the court order was lifted, though, the number of women hired dropped drastically from the 50 percent mandated by the decree to 8.5 percent.[8] Also, the 2000 Status of Women in Policing Survey showed that police agencies without consent decrees had only 9.7 percent sworn female officers, whereas among agencies with the decrees, women represented 14 percent of the sworn officers.[9]

Another example is the Los Angeles Police Department (LAPD), which had been under a consent decree for more than twenty years to recruit more women. It still had not met its goal in 2002, although Mayor Jim Hahn and Chief William Bratton indicated that a plan was in the making to significantly increase the number of female officers. Supposedly the plan would increase the percentage of women to at least 25 percent of the department by targeting recruitment efforts toward women, by mentoring, and by strengthening physical preparation programs. However, as the National Center for Women & Policing (NCWP) showed, although the plan was a good start, it could be improved by overhauling the entry requirements. According the the NCWP, the plan continued "to underemphasize communication skills abilities, and in so doing, wash out qualified female candidates."[10]

While there was evidence that consent decrees were either expiring or simply not being implemented in some agencies, at least minimal recruitment was going forward in many others. In 1991, Susan Erlich Martin analyzed questionnaire responses from 446 police departments which evaluated the effectiveness of affirmative action policies on improving the status of women in policing. The study indicated that affirmative action had made a significant impact on the hiring of females as police officers. The study further found that affirmative action had a considerable impact on "both the proportion of women among applicants and the proportion of female applicants accepted as recruits."[11]

Police departments that already had a woman or two on the force used their success in that area to help provide a "snowball effect" and encourage female candidates. Chief Ella Bully-Cummings agreed that female officers needed to be visible on the street where young women could see them and visualize a career in law enforcement for themselves. "If you can't see it, you can't dream it," she stated.[12]

Some departments used the media to attract qualified candidates; others combed college campuses and connected with female community leaders such as those involved in the YWCA and Girl Scouts to help identify prospects. The St. Louis County Police Department, like many others, used a recruitment poster showing a police woman with the plea to "Become One of the Proud Ones."[13] On the St. Louis poster, however, although the woman was in a police uniform, she was holding the hand of a small female child—a woman in the traditional role of nurturer and caretaker rather than enforcer of the law. (Today, departments recruiting women publish posters and brochures that show women fulfilling all police jobs, including that of a SWAT team member.)

Recruiting females for this nontraditional female job is not always easy, but departments have devised a number of ways to attract women to the profession. Brown and Heidensohn cite comments from several female officers who were successfully recruited into police work.[14] An African American woman explained, "My department was looking for minorities and I kind of doubled up because they were looking for women, and particularly black women." In two jurisdictions, the departments were looking to improve the gender ratio. "I came in at a time when they had a recruitment drive to bring up one policewoman per section . . . there'd only been four women, perhaps 120 guys [then] we were 20." More women victims was the reason for recruitment, according to one female officer: "There were just men; they couldn't handle it properly . . . so it was an outcry from the public."

Nan Hegerty (who would become Milwaukee's Police Chief in November 2002) had tried many nonchallenging jobs. She explained that she was recruited through the media.

> One night I was at home watching TV and here's where my destiny comes in. . . . There was an ad that said, "Be a Milwaukee Police Officer. Women and minorities are encouraged to apply." So I did, and just by my sure [*sic*] willpower made it through the physical agility because I wasn't in very good shape.[15]

Julia Grimes, Director of the Alaska State Troopers, indicated that the agency faced the same difficulties as most of the nation's law enforcement departments—recruiting qualified applicants. "We've been able to fill our academy and keep our positions filled," she stated but added that Alaska's State Police needed "to keep advertising and representing . . . the Alaska State Troopers as a career and an adventure and an opportunity to do things the average person doesn't get to do."[16]

Palo Alto, California, police officer Jean Marie Bready indicated that her department currently recruits but mostly by word of mouth. "We look for established officers in other departments and 'woo' them with the insight of working for a department with a large percentage of women. I think we are currently around 24% female."[17]

Assistant Chief Bonnie Stanton was working as a program manager at a San Francisco rock and roll radio station when a California Highway Patrolman brought in advertising flyers encouraging women to join the California Highway Patrol (CHP). Stanton recalled, "I took one look at the CHP starting salary (which was

$1,259 a month at the time), did the math . . . three times my current salary, and decided to leave the radio station for a career with the CHP."[18]

Deputy Police Chief (retired) Charlene Graham indicated that, although she realized that the job was not for everyone, recruitment had been of great benefit for women. Still, she felt that, in general, recruitment needed to be improved and that it was not all it should be. "The lack of [female] role models out there is a big drawback when it comes to recruiting women. If a department has women successfully filling the job and these women can be seen by those thinking of joining the force, it is a big motivator for anyone who might be hesitant to come on board."[19]

Responding to the authors' 2004 questionnaire (see Appendix 1), New York Sergeant Darlene Rogers emphasized the effect that education may be having on the recruitment of women. She felt that recruitment may not be as effective as in earlier years because today more women are completing college degrees and have many employment opportunities available to them that they might not have had in the past. She indicated that women might rather get a job where they "do not have to put their lives on the line. It's a tough job [policing], and there is little glory."[20]

California Police Chief Lynne Johnson also mentioned danger on the job as a reason women may not pursue a career in law enforcement. She also listed a number of other good reasons: family issues, shift work, close scrutiny by the public, and "up until the last few years, the pay."[21]

Certainly, all of the women's comments show that there are many issues that need to be taken into consideration when an agency is trying to add women to its force. Perhaps one of the best ways, as a 2002 article in *Police Chief* magazine indicated, would be for Police Chiefs simply to reach out to qualified females and let them know that they are welcome and valued. The departments also could perform a statistical analysis of their selection process, by gender, to determine whether something was being done (or not being done) that disproportionately screened women out.[22] (Although the article did not specify the recruitment practices of the Albuquerque and Tucson Police Departments and the Delaware State Police, it might be assumed that they followed the magazine's advice, as they were commended for increasing the percentage of female recruits in their academies.)

JOINING UP

Regardless of family issues, the tough, often dangerous job, the lack of glory, and the financial opportunities open in other fields, many women decide on their own to join police departments. If they are not actively recruited, why do they select the police profession? In films and fiction, a man often does so because his father and grandfather were policemen, and he is only a part of this family of cops. He says something like, "It's just in the blood," or "It's part of our family," or "I always wanted to be like my dad." On the other hand, the female cop never states, "My mom was a cop, so I'm a cop!"

Whether male or female, those who join law enforcement agencies tend do so for a number of reasons other than following in family footsteps. Writing in 1999, Joan Barker mentions that in the older, traditional force (which was almost entirely male in composition), idealism was a major factor—the belief in being able to make a positive change in society. Financial considerations were rarely given then as primary or even secondary motivations. Now new recruits, male and female, focus less on idealistic components and emphasize economic benefits, job security, a stepping-stone to another career, and excitement of the job. Comments from a female officer illustrate both the security and the excitement factor:

> And I got to thinking, working a patrol car . . . you'd never know what you were going to get. Every day would be different, and I need little spurts of adrenaline and excitement during the day. . . . I don't fit the image of what the department wants . . . I mean I know these people who just *live* for the department, twenty-four hours a day . . . but I don't think that it's healthy. You need time off. . . . I won't get rich, but I get enough so I can pay my bills, and go out and have fun vacations and buy neat toys—and have job security.[23]

In a 2003 interview with the authors, Penney S., her long, dark hair neatly held in a French twist, explained that a friend, a policeman, convinced her to apply to the department, as it would be a good job.

> I had known Tim for a number of years; we had been in high school together, but I had been away at college for two years and was just getting back home. Actually, I had never thought of becoming a police officer. I was majoring in psychology but was tired of school. So, when Tim told me that department was looking for women, I decided to apply. He said that he really liked his job and thought there would be good chances for advancement for me as they needed to have some females. The pay was fairly good, and the job provided a pension if you stayed with it long enough. . . . So I guess he sort of recruited me.

Laurie Hadley always wanted to be a cop. She originally was a police woman in Texas and then became a trooper with the Colorado State Patrol. "I work in the canine area," Hadley, a petite blonde, explained. "I work with a black lab named Jack who sniffs for drugs in vehicles. Actually, I'm an instructor for those who work with canines. I'm very happy with my job."[24]

Now in her forties and with almost twenty-two years on the job, one woman who became an officer "did it on a bet." Her high school counselor talked with students about which career path they would take after graduating from high school. She and another girl told the counselor they were going to be cops. He told them to come back and talk with him when they were serious. "So that is when I made up my mind. So I had a bet with the high school counselor. . . . I had to make sure I won the bet."[25]

New Jersey Lieutenant Barbara Steinberg, who had originally been employed as a social worker for the Juvenile Bureau, had no intention of entering the force until being provoked by a negative comment about women in policing.

> In 1978, I was on a panel speaking about drug abuse. When the Chief of Police made a comment he would never hire a woman police officer . . . for the Paramus Police Dept. I just leaned over the dais and said, "I will challenge you, Chief." Everyone laughed. But I passed the tests and was hired. I had no intentions of being a police officer. It

> was a game. I figured I would go to the academy and leave after a while. But little did I realize I fell in love with the job.[26]

Another woman took advantage of funds that became available in the 1970s for law enforcement cadets to attend college if they would serve as police officers. Still another woman needed to be a certified police officer to keep her job in the District Attorney's Office. To become certified she needed to join the police force and attend the police academy. In the end, she did not return to the District Attorney's Office, as she enjoyed police work more than she had anticipated.[27]

Some women were already working in the law enforcement area as civil employees, and when an opportunity opened for them to become sworn officers, they took the challenge. One had a job in the rescue squad and became familiar with police work at accident scenes. Then she was able to be hired as a police dispatcher. "So I saw it kind of from the fire side and the dispatch side and that spurred my interest to go for the deputy sheriff's job."[28]

Charlene Graham also chose her profession. "I was a single mom, working part-time. I had a job that paid more but had no benefits," she explained in an interview over lunch at a local restaurant. "So even though the meter maid job paid less, only $320 a month, it had benefits. When the department announced that they were going to hire female officers, I took the test, passed and became one of the first three women hired in the department in 1972. So it was an accident; it was being in the right place at the right time."[29]

Some women join civilian police departments after serving as military police (MPs). Palo Alto Police Officer Jean Marie Bready began her civilian career after eight years in the navy, which she felt helped shape her future. During that time she had worked as an MP in patrol, in physical security, and in military dog operations as an explosive detection dog handler.

> I chose a law enforcement career for a few reasons. I grew up on a farm with a love of horses. I remember a grade school field trip to the Philadelphia Zoo when I was very young. We saw a police officer on a horse, and I just thought that would be the coolest job ever. And of

> course, growing up watching *The Rookies, Emergency* and *Adam Twelve* just sealed my fate. In California, 1994 was a time when hundreds of people were lining up for police tests.[30]

Even though she chose to join up, Bready mentioned that she would like to see more recruiting by police departments from the military community in order to get strong, independent women to at least consider a police career. She also felt that many women were not attracted to the career because of so much negative publicity about policing in the media and therefore did not consider joining a department.

Like Bready, Vanessa Meade had been in the U.S. Army as an MP. Upon leaving the military, Meade went to college and completed a degree in social work. As a community mental health worker in Homer, Alaska, she frequently went out on crisis calls, which brought her into contact with Alaska's State Troopers. In June 2004, she graduated from the Department of Public Safety Academy in Sitka and went back into police work. "I really missed law enforcement," Mead stated in an interview for the *Homer News*; "I wanted to get back in that."[31]

Another way some enter policing is to first enroll in criminal justice programs, which are now being offered at colleges and universities across the country. Chanda Sommers is taking college courses and entered a police academy in the fall of 2004 in hopes of being a cop. When asked why she had opted to follow this path, she gave a number of reasons:

> I always wanted to be a cop since I was a child. I want to be a good role model for my children. I grew up around cops; my best friend's family were cops. I also need to do something that is exciting. I think it might be hard mentally, but I am a very positive person. Also, I think there needs to be more women as we are more understanding, less physical, more compassionate, more mental and better problem solvers. This college degree will help me meet my goal.[32]

However, deciding to enter the law enforcement profession is only the first step. Next is the sometimes lengthy, and often stressful, selection process.

THE SELECTION PROCESS

Whether they are recruited or choose the profession, before being hired, police officers have gone through various types of assessment, which may vary with the department. Today, some police agencies utilize assessment centers, which provide experienced and trained assessors to evaluate applicants. Usually six to eight exercises are developed that measure the candidates' ability to perform certain tasks needed in the department. Since tasks are different in each department, the exercises must be developed by a trained person and the assessment designed for a particular rank. At present, the Washington Association of Sheriffs and Police Chiefs is one group that contracts with local and state governments to conduct assessment centers.[33] One potential problem with using assessment centers is the lack of funds available in some law enforcement agencies. Therefore, many departments do not hire professional companies but utilize their own personnel for the many components involved in selection.

During the selection process, women, like men, have to pass background checks aimed at uncovering anything in their lives that would make them unacceptable as police officers. Relaxed standards for these searches sometimes are unavoidable if applicants are scarce and demand is high. One LAPD police academy instructor explained the problem sometimes encountered when new recruits were needed:

> We have about a five-hundred-officer attrition rate per year . . . from officers pensioning off, or retiring, or leaving for whatever reason. For the last three years, we've been trying to boost our numbers . . . trying to hire an extra one thousand officers each year. That means we interview and check on forty to fifty thousand applicants to come up with one thousand who get into the academy.[34]

Assuming applicants pass the background search, they must meet certain physical requirements and pass a battery of tests, although these vary slightly depending on the agency. Most departments now require at least two years of college, and some are moving toward hiring only those individuals who have completed a bachelor's degree. Because of these requirements, criminal justice and sociology or criminology degrees are in demand and have been instituted at most community colleges and many universities across the country.

Of course, as with the background checks, if there is a scarcity of applicants for police work, the educational requirements may be waived in some instances. Still, the waiver may be temporary, and the newly hired officers usually are encouraged to enroll in college classes; some departments have resources to fund at least partial tuition and attempt to arrange work schedules to meet class requirements. Overall, in most departments, if there were differences in educational requirements for men and women, they have been eliminated.

In order to learn about state laws and police procedures, police department recruits are required to attend a police academy. This rule also applies to those joining the state police and the sheriff's department. In some states, police academies used to be an integral part of the department, taught by police personnel and often constituting a significant part of that department's budget. However, many of these academies are no longer encompassed within the law enforcement agencies but are now available at community colleges or universities, where students pay to attend. Attending the academy can help prospective recruits understand policing before they take entrance exams. At the same time, agencies save money by not paying wages to recruits while they attend an academy.

Written entrance examinations are usually administered to applicants, although concern remains about the content and validity of some questions, as they may contain gender (or racial) bias and place women at a disadvantage. For example, women tend to do poorly when tested on spatial relations and mechanics. Although police departments needed to demonstrate the job relatedness of the questions, until the 1990s many departments continued to administer entrance examinations that did not meet civil rights criteria unless they were threatened with a lawsuit.[35]

Oral examinations have been and still are administered to potential officers. Penny Harrington (who would rise to the rank of Police Chief) indicated that when she entered the ranks, oral interviews were usually conducted by white, male police officers and recalled that some of the questions she received in the 1970s were blatantly discriminatory. These included "Do you think the men would respect you?" and "Do you really believe that a woman could discipline a man?"[36]

Interviews can be unnerving for anyone, male or female. To make the process fairer for female candidates, agencies could include female officers on the board, give evaluators training in the interview process, and predetermine acceptable questions and answers. Today, most oral exams are conducted by a panel consisting of both men and women. The questions asked tend to be about values, morals, and why the applicant wishes to be in policing. The Albuquerque, New Mexico, Police Department has replaced the board interview with a critical incident interactive video that rates the candidates' responses and has eliminated the gender bias in this phase of their testing. By 2002 the department had increased the number of female recruits in their police academies from 10 percent to 33 percent.[37]

AGILITY TESTING

While oral exams and interviews can be daunting, the biggest problem women faced, as was mentioned in Chapter 1, was the argument that females were not suited for the job because of their physical stature and strength. An article published in a 1929 issue of *Police Journal* illustrates this old debate about women versus men on patrol and is still considered a valid argument in the minds of many.

> There is now almost universal agreement that policewomen should not attempt to do general patrol work. Police work of this type is rather exacting in its physical demands, and men as a sex have greater physical strength and endurance than women as a sex. . . . In view of the general and specific nature of patrol work, the requirements as to strength alone are sufficient to be a determining factor.[38]

Certainly, physical strength and agility are important for police work as they are for many other occupations. The debate seems to be about the amount of strength required and whether physical agility requirements are relevant to police work. Pennsylvania Police Chief Charles Altmiller discussed a rigorous physical test involving jumping over a six-foot wall and dragging a 185-pound dummy for fifty feet, which was implemented by eighty municipalities across Pennsylvania. He was quoted in the *Women and Policing News Wire* as stating that "police chiefs like the new physical fitness test because it's so oriented to police work."[39]

However, police reform advocates have spoken out against the use of police agility testing, finding that the tests lack any relevance to actual police work and tend to eliminate women and small men from the recruit pool.[40] Yet pre-employment agility tests are a big part of the process of becoming a law enforcement officer, even though women tend to be screened out disproportionately. The NCWP suggests that, in addition to basic physical fitness, departments should stress the testing of communication and cognitive skills, which can be a very important part of law enforcement. (For more on this topic, see Chapter 5.)

It is also interesting to note that most departments require agility tests for those *applying* for police jobs and do not test again for the duration of an officer's career. Therefore, an officer could be hired while he or she was in shape but then gain weight or experience other physical challenges that would prevent him or her from passing the test later on. The agility test, then, may be viewed as a method for preventing women from making the force, since it is clearly not a priority for departments once an officer passes the test one time.

Still, with all the controversy about this subject, the 2001 Status of Women in Policing survey indicated that the vast majority of the agencies responding to the survey utilized some form of physical agility testing for entry-level selection. Most of the agencies scored the test on a pass/fail basis, which meant that candidates had to successfully perform the physical agility component before they could move on to the next stage of entry-level selection. The survey also revealed that there was no consensus on the types of physical tests to be used, with some agencies using a timed obstacle course while approximately 30 percent of others utilized running events, a solid wall climb, and push-ups. Some agencies required candidates to take a test of grip strength or trigger pull to measure upper body strength and to exhibit agility when jumping low barriers or hurdles, climbing stairs, and entering or exiting a vehicle.[41]

As was mentioned earlier, many of these physical tests disproportionately affect women negatively when they are vying for positions on a police force. The 2003 report from the NCWP cites material from the Equal Employment Opportunity Commission (EEOC) and explains that an adverse impact of a selection test is established when it is documented that passing rates for women fall below 80 percent of men's. "At that point, the legal burden shifts to the police agency to prove that the test is job related and consistent with business necessity, and that it represents the least discriminatory alternative for selection."[42] The report emphasized that police agencies must remedy the disproportionate negative impact physical agility testing has on women versus men in the selection process, although alternatives or possible remedies are not provided.

At the September 2004 Rocky Mountain Women in Policing Conference, Margaret Moore, Director of the NCWP, discussed one test that many departments still utilize—scaling a six-foot solid wall. When she asked the women and men in her audience to indicate how many of them had the six-foot wall as part of their agility test, numerous hands were raised. This test has always been difficult for women to pass due to the upper-body strength required. As an NCWP report shows, those agencies without physical agility testing (PAT) average 15.8 percent of women as sworn officers; those with PAT have only 10.9 percent.[43]

Moore then pointed out that it was rather absurd to conduct the six-foot-wall test to screen out male or female candidates. An officer scaling a solid wall in pursuit of a suspect, obviously, would be unable to see through or over the wall. Waiting for the officer when he or she landed on the other side could certainly be an armed individual, placing the officer in a dangerous situation.

Questions are also raised about some entry-level tests that require that applicants successfully load an assault rifle or demonstrate that they can physically apprehend a resistant subject. These abilities are "probably best assessed after officers have learned effective techniques as part of their [law enforcement] academy training"[44] instead of being used to screen out applicants who have not needed these skills in their everyday lives.

For example, in 1976, while attending the Memphis Police Academy, Melinda Stroud and Brenda Harris were fired after they failed the firearms and physical tests. Although the Civil Service Commission voted unanimously to reinstate the two as police dispatchers and ordered that they be permitted to try out for the next training class, the two filed suits against the police department. Eventually the suits were settled out of court, with the women graduating from the academy and receiving $2,600 in back pay.[45]

The Memphis academy had signed a consent decree in 1973, committing itself to filling 20 percent of each graduating class with women. If women couldn't meet the physical and firearms standards geared toward males, the academy faced two options: anticipate legal action from the federal government and women who failed the requirements or change the standards to allow more women to graduate. Changes were made to accommodate women candidates, leaving some at the academy concerned that graduates may not have the physical qualifications needed by police officers. As one former officer of the academy stated, "The net result is that a certain number of women are given more slack than the city would like. There are a few women who couldn't even meet women's scores."[46]

In addition to physical strength and handling of guns, height of females also was a major concern of the law enforcement community. It was believed that the height and size of an officer had an effect on the officer's job performance. Supposedly, a tall, large officer would necessarily be a strong person who could command respect from citizens. Because of both strength and respect, the (male) officer would perform the job "more effectively with less 'hassle' from citizens" and therefore would be less likely to be injured or assaulted than a shorter, smaller officer.[47] Therefore, many agencies had height requirements for officers that effectively eliminated both males and females. One woman, who would eventually reach the position of Chief after twenty-one years in law enforcement, recalled her frustration at questions relative to her size during an initial interview for a police job.

> I would say the hardest thing was being taken seriously as a young, petite woman in the middle 70s. I am 5' 2". . . . I remember coming

> home from interviews just really frustrated when I would get questions like, "Gee, were you on the wrestling team? Do you know karate?" Breaking through, I mean we had barely got over height requirements at that time.[48]

Perceptions that size does make a difference have not gone away. A Missouri Police Officer II, working in a department of more than hundred officers with no females in command positions, wrote in 2004 that she continues to get negative comments from the public regarding her height.

> Many times I am sized up on a call because of my height and weight—5 foot 4 inches and 127 pounds. I often hear the comment, "You don't look big enough to be doing this job." There have also been times when I and another female officer have been on a call and asked, "So what do you ladies do when things get bad?"[49]

This officer thought the last question was "funny" as the two were then on a domestic assault call where the male involved (over six feet tall and weighing 185 pounds) had just been "badly assaulted" by his 130-pound wife who was slightly over five feet tall. Apparently the fact that the man had been considerably larger than his spouse had not been to his benefit in this domestic violence incident. The officer felt that these continuing questions about the physical makeup of police women by some citizens "shows the public lacks confidence in female officers. They seem to think if we're not big brutes that we can't handle conflict."[50]

While discriminatory height and weight requirements were finally discarded in the 1970s, today's tests still tend to overemphasize upper-body strength and continue to be a barrier to keep highly qualified women from entering law enforcement. According to the NCWP, studies show that physical prowess is unrelated to job performance. In fact, no research has ever shown that strength is related to an individual's ability to successfully manage a dangerous situation.[51]

An arrest situation encountered in 1977 by Ella Bully-Cummings illustrates that great strength is not always necessary. Bully-Cummings and her male patrol partner attempted to arrest a 6' 5" belligerent drunk suspect. Attempting to put the suspect in handcuffs, her partner was hit in the groin and fell to the ground. Bully-Cummings, who weighed 110 pounds, jumped on the suspect's back and clung to him until additional officers arrived on the scene. "It was kind of hilarious," Bully-Cummings recalled. "My partner went down before me. . . . The suspect told the judge I beat him up."[52]

Whether or not an individual will be successful as a police officer depends on the capabilities of that individual. No one standard can be applied to all female or all male officers. As Joseph Balkin so aptly stated in the *Journal of Police Science and Administration,* "Not all women are able to handle all police jobs—but neither are all men. . . . In some respects, at least, women are better suited for police work than men."[53]

PERSONAL CHARACTERISTICS

In addition to overcoming the stereotype that women are too frail physically to be "good cops," women have had to overcome the view that their personalities are so different from men's that they will be unable to perform at a high level. Certainly, females in American society are generally socialized in a manner different from males. Even today, many females are reared to be fragile, dependent, compliant, cooperative, and nurturant. Conflict, assertiveness, and direct confrontation are not usually a part of their upbringing. Gwendolyn Gerber in her book *Women and Men Police Officers* indicates that "even women who work in highly masculine-typed occupations such as policing are thought to have uniquely 'feminine' qualities such as warmth, concern, and accommodation to others."[54]

According to author Pat Heim, when women become aggressive, no-nonsense, win-at-all costs players, embodying qualities that are thought to be personality characteristics of the male, they are labeled bossy, obnoxious, overbearing, ambitious, or strident bitches who are just "mouthing off." Many times their inputs or achievements are either ignored or summarily dismissed. On the other hand, if females adhere to their socialization and are passive, nurturant, and cooperative in their job setting, they are labeled weak and overly sensitive. Once again, their contributions and successes are ignored or dismissed.[55]

Brown and Heidensohn feel that women have attempted to come to terms with male-dominated police culture in various ways: by seeking approval, by adopting an aggressive style, by resisting the adoption and performance of occupational traits that are masculine, or by retaining as much femininity as the subculture will permit. If overly feminine, the officer risks sexual harassment or may be perceived as ineffectual. If overly masculine traits are adopted, the woman may be denigrated for the loss of femininity and, possibly, perceived as man-hating.[56] The female is caught in a no-win situation. She faces criticism and, possibly, some form of discrimination if she is perceived as too feminine or if she is perceived as too masculine.

One police woman, who would eventually reach the position of Deputy Chief, felt that she had proved her abilities without losing her femininity. "I have always stayed what I think is feminine," she stated. "I never took on a male persona. I think I was strong enough within myself, you know, where I would speak my mind, and I handled myself on the job, and if I had to fight, we fought on the street. . . . I always did my job. . . . I didn't ask the guys, 'Could you do this or would you do this for me?' But that wasn't every female."[57]

Another indicated that if a woman attempted to change her personality to be either too feminine or too masculine in order to try to fit in, she would have problems. "If you are a good, solid person, that is what will come through rather than if you are male or female." Still another woman agreed, stating,

> You got to be who you are. . . . To me, it is a fatal error, particularly for a female officer, to come in and try to [be] something she is not 'cause there is so many obstacles. . . . One is too much stress; you can't carry it off; it seems artificial. . . . When women come in and think they have to be macho, and they have to do this job the way they perceive a man does the job, it is not natural for them and they are not successful.[58]

Captain Margaret T. also felt that a police woman did not have to be "one of the boys or act like one of them. You can still be a female and respected," she stated. Lieutenant Barbara Steinberg agreed with this statement. "Be yourself. Do not be one of the guys."[59]

Sergeant Rogers made a good point when she indicated that a woman needed to be both "independent and interdependent. Being a team player is a must," she said, "but not to the extent that you jeopardize your ethics." She explained that a police woman had to be able to make independent decisions but also had to be able to "work well with her colleagues."[60]

Women emphasized that in addition to the expected characteristics of any police officer—honesty, integrity, ethics, and commitment—stamina, a thick skin, a sense of humor, and tenacity were important elements of being effective on the job. One felt that a sense of humor was necessary because in some situations "you really have to laugh at yourself." Another female officer answered a questionnaire and provided a list of qualities a woman needed to bring to her job: assertiveness, intelligence, confidence, good work ethic, flexibility, good communication skills, and ability to be a team player. A New Jersey Lieutenant of Detectives who asked that her name not be used also feels that, while she doesn't want to be one of the guys, she does "want to be one of the team. I make it clear that although I might not agree with male dominated attitudes, there are things that I can learn from these attitudes. I also believe that women have the ability to multi-task and conduct several assignments at one time." Still another felt that tenacity was necessary because there would be times when duties would be difficult and challenging.[61] In cases like this, commitment to one's career or goals would help one cope with challenges in the work environment.

Some traditional officers in the LAPD (those hired during a time when the force consisted primarily of white males) reported being concerned about the lack of commitment by newer recruits. One police woman was extremely negative when she discussed more recent female hires. "The females are just here to find husbands. I wouldn't want to work with them. They're not here to do police work.... They're not cops. I swear. I won't work with any of them."[62]

Officer Bready realized that this could be a common complaint from older, more traditional personnel. She emphasized that in order to be equal to her male counterpart, a woman needed to view herself "as a police officer, not a *female* police officer. [She] must be an equal that the male counterparts have faith in."[63] Darlene Rogers also emphasized that a female needs to "remember that she is a woman doing a job, that of a police officer."[64] The majority of police women would agree with Bready and Rogers; their commitment to their careers is paramount, and they are interested in doing a good job for the public as they try to "fit in."

It should also be mentioned that the gender composition of a department could be a factor in whether females are accepted or not. If a department didn't have any females already, the new "woman on the block" might have to fight all the prejudices against a female cop before being accepted.

> When I came here this was a pretty small police department . . . maybe 18 of us all together. I found out four years later that the males thought that the day I walked through the door, their world was coming to an end. But I've never had a problem actually. I would have to say that maybe being a female was an advantage. I was treated just about like any other officer.[65]

Another woman echoed the same sentiments. "We were small back then. We worked 12-hour shifts . . . two on a shift. We had to work pretty independently, so it didn't take long before you either had to do it or not. And they [male officers] figured out that you could do the job. . . . They were not overly protective.[66]

If the department had a significant number of women officers (and possibly a female or two in top-ranking positions), the way had been paved for new women entering the ranks. Usually, the female only needed to prove that she could be a "good cop."

MENTORING

Regardless of whether they were in small or large departments, most of the women interviewed felt they were in the right career for them. They were quick to point out that part of this satisfaction was due to support from family members, friends, and colleagues. One method that has been of great help in assisting women entering law enforcement is mentoring, where two people have a working relationship and one acts as a counselor or patron to the other. The mentor is usually a senior colleague who can use his or her skills and experience to help the new recruit.

Since it is felt that, in general, women and minorities have greater difficulty finding mentors, some law enforcement departments have instituted mentoring programs. According to a 1998 International Association of Chiefs of Police survey, 13 percent of the eight hundred agencies surveyed reported that they had formal mentoring programs. These programs partnered newly hired women police officers with senior or command officers, male or female, in order to create a supportive environment.[67]

Mentoring can be a simple, one-on-one interaction or it can come from informal networks. "I've been a mentor for younger officers who come into the Police Force, and, informally, I'm a mentor, together with another woman, for the other females who come in," stated one female officer.[68] Some women have met at conventions or seminars and set up networks to discuss similar problems and help each other—a sort of therapy for what Brown and Heidensohn label "female cop culture."

Because policing is still a male-dominated field, Lieutenant Deborah J. Cady (from a department of more than hundred officers with only eight women) believes that "female officers frequently feel a little more isolated on the job as male officers may be slower to accept them as equals and welcome them into their group."[69] Mentoring by other officers could help these females become integrated into a peer group.

Officer Jean Marie Bready indicated that she had been "mentored by a female sergeant in the past and was currently being mentored by a male lieutenant. I have not been a mentor per se but would certainly make myself available if in the position of leadership."

Patrol Officer Kristin Touchstone is the first and only woman in a department of twenty-seven, including the Chief. "I had a Field Training Officer for three months when I first started," Touchstone explained, "but I have not mentored anyone." Still another officer considered her first Chief to be one of her mentors and has had several male officers who she "looked up to and learned from."[70]

Several women interviewed could not recall having mentors but stated that they were either mentoring at the present time or would be willing to act as mentors.

Regardless of the problems females encountered, they have breached the blue wall. They have joined law enforcement ranks in ever greater numbers since the middle of the last century and have held their own in this heavily male profession. Still, as the following incident shows, some citizens become disconcerted when they call for help and the responding cop turns out to be a "fragile" female instead of the stereotypical burly male. Working in a small town where citizens did not often encounter female officers, Sergeant Jennifer Mykonos realized she had to be sensitive to how people saw her. One time an elderly woman had locked her keys in her car and had frantically called for police aid. When Mykonos responded to the call and tried to help her, the woman asked what she was doing. The last thing she had expected was that the "cop" would be a woman. "She was not fully comfortable with me," Mykonos indicated.[71] However, when at a later date the same woman called the department for another reason, she specifically *asked* for Sergeant Mykonos.

CHAPTER 3

Facing Challenges

> Sometimes it gets down to the nitty-gritty and I don't want some cute 120-pound blonde working with me.
>
> —Memphis Police Captain, *Memphis Press-Scimitar*, 1980

Although law demanded that women be permitted into the police ranks as full-fledged sworn officers, those women who began their careers in the last century were truly pioneers in the masculine-oriented police subculture. Unique entities in their respective agencies, they faced a number of obstacles, not the least of which was male officers' negative attitudes toward them. For example, male officers in the LAPD formed a clandestine organization called Men against Women. Its purpose was to wage an orchestrated campaign of ritual harassment, intimidation, and even criminal activity against women officers.[1] Acceptance from male colleagues was a slow, gradual process, as most men felt that female officers could not handle the macho world of policing. Eventually, even minimal acceptance came about only through the legal system.

As mentioned in Chapter 2, studies in the 1980s (among them those by Martin, Remington, Bell, and Lieberman) stressed the belief that female officers were not considered to be capable of performing the duties of a police officer as well as their male counterparts and that women would have to rely on their male partners to gain citizen compliance and to maintain control. Lieberman's later study demonstrated that men *and* women both rated men as performing better in their fields than women, even if the work was identical.[2] Possibly the biggest question facing the future of women in policing, especially in large metropolitan areas, was, Would male officers accept women as partners when the two-person team would have to meet the dangers of patrol every day?

GAINING TRUST

Climbing into a patrol car with a male colleague did not necessarily mean that a woman had gained credibility as a full-fledged officer. Men often were confused as to how to treat their female partners and, assuming it was expected, would open the car doors for them or try to protect them. Occasionally, the males simply dismissed the women as unimportant. Lynne Johnson (who would eventually rise to the position of Police Chief) recalls an incident early in her career that, she felt, was indicative of the way some male officers responded to females on the force. In one incident, Johnson and another female officer responded to a report that an armed man was threatening to commit suicide. A male officer also answered the call for help, but when he saw the two women, he said, "Just my luck; two female cops." Immediately, he turned and simply walked away.[3] The women were taken aback somewhat but handled the situation successfully and professionally.

Occasionally the male officer would merely try to push the female into the background when they responded to a call. Finding a jumper about to leap from a bridge, one man told his partner, "Here, hold my hat while I rush him." The woman, irritated by this dismissal, replied, "Hold you own damn hat" and went to the jumper's aid.[4]

Men tended to cite safety issues as their prime concern with female officers. Whether or not the female would be able to back up her male partner in a violent encounter was (and for some still is) a big question. Some males refused to partner with a female, and one male's statement in the 1980s pretty much summed up the problem females faced.

> I don't think they should be on this job, not in uniform, not working with me. I want somebody who can back me up. . . . I don't want someone I have to back up. There's only one woman I'd work with in this district . . . 'cause she's meaner than most guys I've seen on the street. . . . When I get into fights it's usually several against me and I'd rather be by myself. That way I don't have to watch out for her.[5]

Generally, the men felt that in a physically dangerous situation, the females would be unable to defend themselves or their partners. The men wanted a partner who would be "tough," but men felt that women were not supposed to be tough. The males relied heavily on male partners for protection when needed, a sort of male camaraderie that bound them together. To have to depend on a woman was considered by some to be unmanly and humiliating. A man wanted to be able to depend on his partner but not to have to depend on a woman.[6]

Reflecting at the end of his career, one officer probably summed up most male officers' feelings about female patrol partners in the 1970s and 1980s:

> I was one of the ones that didn't want to see it—women on patrol, and I'm still not really comfortable with it because I'm just a traditional guy . . . but the fact is that back when this was evolving early on, we thought there was gonna be all kinds of violence, the women were gonna get their ass kicked. . . . When you have somebody's sister or mother in the car with you, getting out there and doing that macho man thing is just not the thing to do, because your're eventually responsible for what you start. . . . So if you're a combat veteran and the guy next to you is a Marine, and he's a combat veteran, well you know what the hell's going on and if you start something, you know you're gonna finish.[7]

However, seldom did the dire events that were envisioned by this officer come to pass, and the officer grudgingly admitted that women had been of benefit to the department: "The society evolved along with the police department, and women seem to be functioning quite well. They seem to be much more of an asset than a liability. . . . Women have civilized police work in Los

Angeles to a great degree over the years, and I can't say that it was unwarranted. It was something that needed to happen."[8]

Of course, not all problems with the partnering of a male and a female were due to physical abilities and possible violent confrontations. Frequently, when a man and woman were paired in an automobile for an eight-hour shift, spousal jealousy reared its head. "Too close for comfort" is the feeling many wives gave when asked how they felt about their husbands sharing a police car with a female officer month after month. In the Dallas Police Department the wives of male officers protested the presence of female officers. At a Police Association meeting an older women vehemently stated, "We want this organization to do something about our husbands having to work with women. Women are going to get them killed or they're going to be cheating on us. . . . If women want to be on the police force, by God, they ought to work together."[9]

One female officer, who was married, did not have children, and had been in law enforcement for more than twenty years, indicated that while the wives of the men had included in their comments to the Chief that they did not want the Chief to hire her because they felt that she would not be able to back up their husbands in a dangerous situation, there was the other, more personal reason. "Not being able to act as backup was the reason they gave," she stated. "But I think they just didn't want their husbands riding around for hours in a car with another female. I became a threat to their marriages."[10]

Overall, police women interviewed felt that jealousy of wives could be a factor but said they could handle this issue. Of course, as one stated, "If you are constantly in close contact with a guy for eight hours a day or longer, you both get to know each other very well. Sure, something romantic can develop, but I've been [on patrol] with several different men, and we were just two officers doing our job."

A New Jersey Lieutenant of Detectives pointed out that the "one thing I have strived to do during my career is always getting to know the wives of the officers I work with. I want them to know me and that I am not a threat. I make my family a priority in my life and let my officers know that they should, too." By doing this she was able to circumvent a possible jealousy issue.

On the flip side, there are instances where husbands may become jealous of their wives' male partners. Susan Ehrlich Martin indicates that several women acknowledged that their husbands or boyfriends were jealous at their being constantly in the company of men or at their working at night with a male partner. One female officer noted that while her husband liked her monthly paycheck, he "adamantly insists that she come straight home after work."[11] However, none of the women interviewed by the authors indicated that they had jealousy issues with their significant others. In fact, almost all of them stressed the amount of support given to them by family members, including husbands.

Also, it should be pointed out that the budgets of many departments preclude having two officers in a car. In this case, the problem of a female or male officer being constantly in close contact with someone else's spouse never occurs. Issues other than this become much more important to the police woman and to the department as a whole.

HARASSMENT

Probably the biggest problem women entering law enforcement have to face is sexual harassment. Sexual harassment is a form of discrimination that violates Title VII of the Civil Rights Act of 1964 and can be broken down into three categories: hostile environment, quid pro quo sexual harassment, and gender harassment. A hostile environment is one in which there is any behavior that would interfere with an individual's work performance or creates an offensive, intimidating, or hostile work environment. Contributing to a hostile environment would be behavior such as offensive jokes, cartoons, or posters; requests for dates or sexual favors; references to body parts; and physical contact that interferes with an individual's job performance. The harassment must be unwelcome but may occur without economic injury to a victim. The victim or the harasser may be a man or woman and does not have to be of the opposite sex. The harasser can be a supervisor, a coworker, or a nonemployee. Also, the victim does not have to be only the person being harassed but may be anyone affected by the offensive conduct.[12]

Quid pro quo sexual harassment includes unwelcome sexual advances or requests for sexual favors and verbal or physical conduct of a sexual nature that explicitly or implicitly implies that an individual will be given a job benefit in return for a sexual favor.[13] "Something for something" is a term often used to explain this type of sexual harassment. For example, if an individual complies with a request, that person will get a promotion, a good job evaluation, a better office, or some other "perk."

In the 1960s, when the Civil Rights Act was passed, probably few women in any type of employment said much about sexual harassment. In the 1960s and 1970s, police women simply handled harassment in different ways. Some ignored it; some confronted it; some didn't even recognize it was happening. One woman explained, "Back then it was an accepted thing. It was not something that I necessarily would even have thought of . . . jokes, wisecracks, those types of things. That was back in 1974; we hadn't even heard of it."[14]

"I'm not sure it existed as such," another woman explained. "It was just there, a part of being female. If a coworker put his arms around you or patted you on the fanny, you didn't say or do anything, especially if you were on your own and didn't have any other means of supporting yourself. You needed the money. You may not have liked it, all that touching, but it just went with the job. You didn't think much about it."

Still others spoke of their departments in the 1970s when for most women there "wasn't something called sexual harassment."

> I mean you would have people that would hit on you, that would ask you out, or they would make comment[s], but that was pre-enlightenment. . . . I mean there was an incident once where . . . I was still pretty young on the job, like my second or third year. . . . And when we came in that night someone had put like a Playboy bunny picture up on the board and said this is the female summer uniform. But I am telling you, I took them to task. I said if I saw any-more crap like that I was going to turn it into internal affairs. . . . We never found out who it was, and they thought it was amusing . . . just a joke and fun.[15]

Chief Penny Harrington also gave an interesting example of her introduction to the police environment when she was hired by the Portland Police Bureau around that time.

> During a self-defense class, I was supposed to throw this guy who was highly trained in one of the martial arts. . . . He grabbed me from behind—but as I turned to throw him, he grabbed my sweatshirt and pulled it over my head. I stood there in my bra, totally embarrassed, while the class laughed and laughed. To me it was horseplay.[16]

Harrington went on to say that such an action was similar to what she had seen while in college but emphasized that she wouldn't look at the incident in the same manner today.

Women were pushing for changes, however, and in *Ellison v. Brady* (1991), the court applied what is known as the "reasonable woman" standard. This rule stated, "We hold that a female plaintiff states a prima facie case of hostile environment sexual harassment when she alleges conduct which a reasonable woman would consider sufficiently severe or pervasive to alter the conditions of employment and create an abusive working environment."[17]

While this seems to offer protection to victims, when individuals complain of harassment, they may find little support, as police departments often have an unwritten rule of silence with regard to officers' conduct. Colleagues who had been friendly and supportive may distance themselves. The perpetrator of the offense may become covertly even more offensive. The supervisor, who may not want the department's image tarnished, may be reluctant to push forward an investigation. If the victims win in an investigation, they may find they are not desired as partners or are not able to get transferred to another area. In other words, they become pariahs in the police force.

If a case goes to court, proving (or refuting) a claim of sexual harassment also can be very difficult as, according to S. E. Burns' 1995 research, it can place the victim of the harassment on trial, similar to a rape victim. Burns indicates that the plaintiff is

> routinely required to explain why, if she was being subjected to sexual harassment, consistent with the claim of unwelcomeness, she

failed to complain, remained politely silent, appeared flattered, joked, or even affirmatively participated in reciprocal slurs.[18]

These may be among the reasons why studies cited on the Internet from the *Women & Policing News Wire* reveal that of the approximately 80 percent of women police officers who have been subjected to sexual harassment at some time in their careers, very few file formal complaints, as they do not wish to suffer repercussions. According to Penny Harrington, women who have formally complained have been falsely accused of crimes such as child abuse and drug violations, threatened with death, and not backed up in emergencies. Jamila Bayati, who left her position as a Los Angeles Sheriff's Deputy after filing a sexual harassment complaint, indicated that complaining was usually the last resort for women officers, since doing so would likely end their careers or make their lives intolerable.[19]

However, as the following cases show, a growing number of women apparently have decided to risk their careers and bring charges against their alleged harassers. For example, Massachusetts State Police Lieutenant Rosemarie Murphy and Detective Lieutenant Paula Loud filed a suit in which they alleged that the agency was deliberately hindering women's opportunities for promotion. The suit also claimed that the department waited for a promotion list in which the names of the two females did not appear to fill eight new Captain slots—all with males. In another lawsuit, three California female officers were awarded $3.5 million after a jury found that the police department failed to prevent sexual harassment and created a hostile work environment.[20]

In a case that was unresolved at the time of this writing, State Trooper Jody A. Reilly, the first and only female helicopter pilot in the Massachusetts State Police, filed a harassment complaint in January 2004, the thirtieth such claim filed since 1995. According to the Massachusetts Commission against Discrimination, Reilly has accused her supervisor, Lieutenant Michael Barry, with "making repeated sexual overtures since she was assigned to the Air Wing four years ago."[21]

Another sexual harassment suit ended with the Chief's resignation from the Cosmopolis, Washington, Police Department (although he gave as his reason declining health). Officer Shellee Stratton and administrative clerk Shelley Willet—the only two women in the department—claimed that the chief had sexually harassed them and filed the charges in April 2002 with the federal EEOC.[22]

A 2002 article from the *Women & Policing News Wire* relates the case of Roberta Kramarski, who was fired from the force before finally winning her lawsuit. In July 1999 Kramarski filed a federal lawsuit against the Oakland Park, Illinois, Police Department, alleging "that she was harassed with derogatory comments, was not given adequate back-up by fellow officers on dangerous jobs, and was passed over for special assignments." Even though the Illinois Appellate Court ruled that Kramarski was wrongfully fired, it took her three years and a ruling by the Illinois Supreme Court to be reinstated.[23] It is ironic that one of her first duties was to attend a seminar on discrimination and sexual harassment.

In general, however, departments are finding it more difficult to ignore this problem than was the case in earlier years.

GENDER HARASSMENT (DISCRIMINATION)

In addition to sexual harassment, problems arise for police women simply because of their gender. As women entered police departments, they encountered issues that some might think of as unimportant but that made the job considerably more difficult or stressful. For example, until the late 1980s, uniforms designed specifically for women were not available, so police women wore street clothes or their own skirts and male officers' uniform shirts. This lack of a uniform set them apart from the males and often kept them from being identified as police officers by the public.[24]

Another problem was the lack of adequate lavatory facilities for women. Most police buildings had a locker room for the men, but the needs of female officers were given little or no consideration. In *Breaking and Entering*, Connie Fletcher cites a woman who recalled that in 1986 she was in a district that did have a locker room for women, but all of the lockers were already in use. No additional lockers were added, so she had to keep all of her equipment—uniform, raincoat, any papers—in the trunk of her car. Another female officer recalled that she used a small closet in front of the unisex bathroom to store her gear. Still another, who was the first woman on the SWAT team in her district, was fortunate to be in a department where there was a women's locker room. She could get dressed there, but her bag of equipment was stored in the men's locker room. To get the bag she had to knock on the men's door and ask to be admitted or get one of the men to bring out her equipment so she could be ready for duty.[25]

For Officer Michelle Sherwood of Port Chester, New York, sixteen years passed before the department built a women's locker room. Newly hired male officers were provided with facilities, but female needs either were not given any consideration or simply were felt to be unimportant.

> These things are the things that make you know if you are accepted or not. I mean if you don't have a locker room that you could go change to and you . . . wait 16 years, and some rookie who walks in and he has a locker room, how does that make you feel? You don't feel good.[26]

These conditions still exist in some police buildings today, which means that the female officer has to locate another area where she can get ready for duty. While some may think these are petty grievances, they are demeaning and make the work environment more uncomfortable and give the feeling of less acceptance.

Other types of workplace problems (or comments of a nonsexual nature) that indicate unequal treatment in the work environment based on one's sex or gender and that demean women also are categorized as "gender discrimination." The NCWP lists seven areas that fall into this category:

1. Women being assigned to "traditionally women's jobs" such as child abuse, juveniles, sex crimes, domestic violence, and school programs and being prevented from assignments to SWAT teams, homicide, gang units, and the like
2. Tests for promotions or other job opportunities that are not job related and that result in women not getting promoted at the same rate as men
3. Women receiving more severe discipline than men for similar misconduct

4. Women being disciplined for behaviors for which men are not even investigated
5. Women being held to a higher or different level of performance on performance evaluations
6. Women not being given equal consideration for specialized training, conferences, specialty job assignments, and the like
7. Pregnant women not given light duty when men injured off-duty are given lighter assignments[27]

Discrimination on the basis of pregnancy, childbirth, or a related medical condition falls under the heading of discrimination on the basis of gender. According to the NCWP, one of the concerns most frequently raised by pregnant officers is knowledge about department policies regarding pregnancy. The NCWP has written a guide ("Recruiting and Retaining Women: A Self-Assessment Guide for Law Enforcement") that indicates that agencies are not providing employees with adequate information and that some agencies have unlawfully discriminated against pregnant employees. Although the 1993 Family and Medical Leave Act (FMLA) established federal minimum leave requirements for private, state, and local government workers, apparently some departments have neglected to provide pregnant officers with specific policies, such as notification procedures, availability of light duty assignments, maternity uniforms, leave benefits, and so forth.[28]

According to the NCWP, one of the most frequent questions received at the center is from women who are pregnant and who may have medical conditions related to their pregnancy. The center emphasizes that these women should be treated no differently than other persons not so affected but who may be similar in their ability or inability to work, including any who may become ill or injured in off-duty accidents. Also stressed is the fact that "employers are prohibited from forcing a pregnant employee to take disability leave as long as the employee is still physically fit to work. Employers may not alter a woman's assignment against her will based on her pregnancy if that decision is based on stereotypes about what kind of work pregnant women should do or on concerns about how the public or other officers will react to a pregnant officer."[29]

These rules are not always followed, however. Sometimes when an officer notifies the agency that she is pregnant, she may be removed from her duty position; often no effort is made to find her some type of light duty. If such a position is available, some male officers may be unhappy about the new assignment. One male who had particularly strong feelings that women should not be permitted in the ranks felt that women used pregnancy as an excuse to get softer jobs than men got. Sergeant Darlene Rogers recalled that when she first started work, her field training officer bluntly stated, "You don't belong here. I don't agree with women being on the job. All they do is get pregnant and then look for a job inside the building."[30] He felt that the men end up doing the real police work while the pregnant women get the breaks.

During various seminars at the September 2004 Rocky Mountain Women in Policing Conference, several women related stories of employment problems encountered due to their pregnancies. When Marilyn D. became pregnant, she was demoted from her patrol job, put on desk duty, and had her salary reduced. Another woman explained that her Chief had called her into his office and said she no longer had a job. He did tell her, "If a position is available after you have the baby, we will consider rehiring you."

Times are changing, however, and departments can no longer discriminate on this issue without possibly facing lawsuits. For example, in 2002 four Massachusetts state troopers were awarded more than a million dollars in damages from a lawsuit charging pregnancy discrimination. The charges were based on a 1997 directive that prohibited pregnant officers from "wearing uniforms, interacting with the public, working overtime and driving police cruisers."[31]

Of course, pregnancy is only one of the reasons lawsuits are filed. Various incidents of gender discrimination can prompt police women to look for redress in the courts. A suit filed by officers Arin Reining and Nina Murphy against the police department in Sumner, Washington, alleged that the two were discriminated against because of their sex and then faced retaliation when they made complaints. The two also alleged that Sumner's Police Chief singled them out for discipline and told one of them that she would never be promoted "because a high-ranking woman would embarrass the department." Although Murphy remained with the department as its only female officer, Reining resigned and took a position as a Deputy with the Benton County Sheriff's Department.[32]

Kathleen Stefani, a twenty-five-year veteran of the Massachusetts State Police, also filed a suit claiming gender discrimination. She became one of seven female troopers to file complaints with the Massachusetts Commission against Discrimination in 2002 and 2003. According to an article in the *Boston Globe*, Stefani had been demoted to the rank of Captain after she permitted a woman's advocacy group to recommend her (and other women) to Massachusetts Governor Mitt Romney for a high-level appointment. In her complaint Stefani alleged that her boss, the state Police Superintendent, told her that she "should never have sent [her] resume to the Governor's Committee" and that she "was disloyal for doing so."[33]

Unfortunately, those who file complaints often have a difficult time with supervisors or may find that their coworkers distance themselves from the whistle-blower for fear of appearing to agree with the complaints or for fear of retaliation. While officials at the Massachusetts State Police headquarters would not comment on Jody Reilly's allegations, Reilly indicated that false rumors had been circulating among her colleagues and felt that her reputation had been damaged. "My training, credentials, licensure, and qualifications as a pilot have been unfairly criticized," Reilly stated in her complaint, "and I have been shunned by my supervisors and coworkers."[34]

Milton, Massachusetts, Police Officer Joyce Donlon continued to be on suspension as of March 2004 due to a lawsuit alleging gender discrimination. According to Donlon, she was called into Chief Kevin Mearn's office to discuss her performance. However, Donlon states that the Chief discussed her off-duty conduct, having coffee with her partner, Sergeant John King. According to Donlon, Mearn chastised her, saying, "You are a married woman. You shouldn't be having coffee with male officers."[35] (The Santa Barbara suit filed by Smith and Hause also indicated that the two officers had suffered retaliation for their actions.)[36]

Occasionally, those who file discrimination lawsuits come out winners. In Santa Barbara, California, a jury awarded $3.2 million in compensatory and punitive damages to Sergeant Juanita Smith and Officer Margaret Hause. The Santa Barbara Police Department was accused of sex discrimination, gender-based harassment, failure to prevent discrimination, and retaliation. The case alleged that the agency had never promoted a women in its 102-year history.[37]

In many instances, women felt that the discrimination had only become more subtle, less overt than in the past—had "gone underground." For example, as one female indicated in Gossett and Williams' study, "It is not the department hiring you and saying you are going to be put in juvenile, or the only thing you can investigate is sexual assaults because that is where you can do that better than a male officer."[38] It is the continuing implication that there are certain police jobs that are basically suited for females rather than males.

Talking with some male officers can turn out to be a problem. In a 2004 interview, one female Sergeant, who asked not to be identified by name, was investigating a case and went with a male detective to speak with a male Sergeant in another city.

> I would talk to him. He would answer to my detective. He would not look at me during the whole conversation, which was about thirty minutes in length. I had faced this problem before, so I didn't let it bother me. But my detective was furious. He asked how I could stand to be treated like that by another officer. I just shrugged and said, "Been there, done that."

Another indicated that the discrimination was not something that occurred on a daily or routine basis. It was not blatant but subtly gave advantages to male over female officers. Female officers were not taken seriously, with males often not acknowledging them, especially if they were in supervisory positions. "They [male officers] . . . know that I am the sergeant. They should come to the sergeant first and then up the chain of command. They will look and see me and see him [the male lieutenant] and will walk directly into his office."[39]

A letter published in *Police Review* in July 1997 sums up the same age-old rhetoric against gender equality and leaves a negative feeling about the effectiveness of the concept of equality.

> As far as discrimination goes, you will never completely eradicate it—the nature of mankind is too complex for that. The good Lord in his wisdom made male and female different. Most people accept that. The male is traditionally the provider and it is feasible that this could be a reason why there are not so many women who reach high rank in the [police] service. It is not anything to do with discrimination, but rather the desire many women have to curtail careers to concentrate on a role as mother and wife.[40]

RACE DISCRIMINATION

Women are not only harassed sexually or because of their gender; they may also face discrimination due to their race (and many times a combination of both of these). In cities with a population of 250,000 or more, statistics from the U.S. Department of Justice in the 1990s indicated that blacks comprised 17.2 percent of all police officers. Although statistics vary regarding the number of blacks in the female police force, Susan E. Martin indicated in 2004 that "women of color now comprise almost half (47.5 percent) of all women police officers."[41] However, the barriers to acceptance and equality in policing are still faced by both African American men and women. Because they are still relatively sparse in number compared to whites, they may be viewed as being hired to fill quotas or as "tokens" and may be treated in a different manner by the numerically dominant group. "Due to their visibility, tokens face extra performance pressures, exclusion, and stereotypic treatment by those around them."[42]

Most studies regarding African American police personnel have been conducted on men; however, with an increase in minority officers from 1978 to 1986, more studies involving women were undertaken. For example, as might be expected, a larger percentage of black women than white women reported being victims of both race and sex discrimination. Some felt that those they worked with felt they knew less, and therefore they had to work twice as hard to prove they were capable.[43]

Martin also indicates that when on street patrol, white women were more likely to be protected by both white and black men than were black women by both white and black men. This was due to a number of reasons—fewer black male officers, pressure by white officers not to back up the women, and the belief that women should not be on patrol. The unique effect of race and sex produced ambiguity with respect to just which type of discrimination a woman was facing. "Sometimes I couldn't tell if what I faced was racial or sexual or both," a female officer stated, " 'cause the Black female is the last one on the totem pole in the department."[44] (Because of the combination of the effects of race and gender, African American women often face multiple disadvantages—a phenomenon labeled "double jeopardy" or the "double whammy.")

Another woman, a black female supervisor, realized that her problem with a subordinate involved both sex and race. She had a white male subordinate who deliberately did not follow procedures when she was his boss and, after being transferred, gave his new male supervisor problems. "So it wasn't a female thing," she is cited as saying, "but at the time I couldn't be sure. . . . I felt he was rebelling against me because I was a female lieutenant and a Black lieutenant. I had a double whammy on me as female and Black."[45]

The question arises as to why African American women were interested in policing if they had to face the problems of prejudice and discrimination. First, law enforcement was an attractive option compared to jobs traditionally open to them. Sokoloff, Price, and Kuleshnyk found in a 1992 study that, even though they acknowledged that there was discrimination in policing, this was also the case for jobs outside that environment. For them, policing offered fairly good wages, good benefits, fairly steady employment, and "clear rules for promotion."[46] Also, as with white women, affirmative action recruiting messages drew them into the field. Finally, according to Martin and Jurik, black women were activists and leaders in the black community. Entering law enforcement enabled black women "to wield authority in the African-American community and to work to alter an organization often viewed as oppressive."[47]

SEXUAL ORIENTATION DISCRIMINATION

Although federal law covers race discrimination, using standards similar to those for sexual harassment and gender discrimination, it does not prohibit discrimination or harassment because of an individual's sexual orientation unless the individual is a federal worker.[48] To avoid harassment and discrimination, until approximately fifteen years ago, gay men and lesbians in all career fields kept their sexual orientation hidden and, usually, undetected. This was also the case for those working in law enforcement.

In a 2004 study by Susan L. Miller, Kay B. Forest, and Nancy C. Jurik, officers who remained closeted felt that disclosure involved both safety and trust issues. In other words, they thought they might be physically abused or that needed police backup would be slow in coming. They also felt that coworkers might withdraw their support and that in the eyes of the community, their moral authority would be diminished.[49]

However, in 1992, a police officer for the first time publicly acknowledged his sexual orientation, and a year later, another gay officer became the first to "come out" while serving on the NYPD.[50] Today, some cities have gay-sensitive police chiefs. For example, former Police Chief Bernard Parks of the LAPD indicates that his department has dozens of sworn and civilian personnel who openly identify themselves as lesbian or gay. He also indicated that as police chief he had "made it quite clear that gay and lesbian officers will not be treated as second-class citizens by anybody under my command."[51]

This does not mean that homosexual officers are accepted in the ranks by all their colleagues. Concerns are raised regarding morality and possible negative effects on department morale. While some are outspoken about their sexuality, others tend to lead double lives, marry a member of the opposite sex, or create fictional relationships with the opposite sex for protection. Even today, many gay men and lesbians in law enforcement are hesitant to declare their sexual orientation due to "fears of rejection, of being the butt of jokes and pranks, of being victims of overt harassment and discrimination, and of not being backed up on calls." Some have been beaten or blackmailed, or have received death threats.[52]

Miller, Forest, and Jurik indicated that every lesbian officer in their sample stated that they had seen antigay cartoons and graffiti on bulletin boards and in the locker room. They felt that they had been excluded from informal social events and from the grapevine gossip normally found in work environments. In addition, they "had heard or been the target of antigay or antilesbian jokes or derogatory slang."[53]

Some women in policing have experienced enough indications of gay prejudice (homophobia) or what they consider overt discrimination to become involved in lawsuits against various departments. Sue Herold, a nine-year veteran of law enforcement, joined Officer Mitch Grobeson's lawsuit against the LAPD for the manner in which it treated lesbian and gay officers. Herold does not feel that the LAPD has changed much in regard to gay officers. She also indicated that she did not get any support from other gay cops because "if you hang out with Sue, it's guilt-by-association." She also does not recommend law enforcement as a career for lesbians.

> It's a neat job, but the decision needs to be given a lot of thought by a young gay or lesbian, because this is a profession that for years to come is going to be dominated by macho, chauvinistic, egotistical, and sometimes racist men. They'd be crazy unless they gave it a lot of serious thought and had no other way to earn a living. . . . The only thing I know how to do is to be a cop. This is all I'm trained to do.[54]

A ten-year officer and street supervisor with the Madison, Wisconsin, police department, Cheri Maples explained that in the police academy, she didn't let anyone know that she was a lesbian. There was what she called a "button campaign" directed against lesbians, with the future officers wearing buttons that said "Straight as an arrow" or "Happily hetero." Maples did find that later on some of her colleagues began to understand that she wasn't "a heck of a lot different from them" and became more accepting of her as just another officer. Still, she continued to encounter hostility from many.

> There's one guy who won't even grunt at me if I say hello. I don't get comments to my face because they know I won't tolerate it—I would have written people up for that. But behind my back, definitely. I don't want to imply that Madison is this great place where there is absolutely no price to be paid for being out [of the closet]. . . . A lot of times I feel more exposed than I want to feel. I always feel like, "Why

> do I have to be making these choices to be out and visible, and why can't some other people help a little bit more."[55]

On the other hand, Travis County, Texas, Sheriff Margo Frazier tends to disagree with Herold. An openly lesbian woman herself, Frazier (one of just 21 female county Sheriffs out of some 3,200 in the United States) is head of a 1,200-person department and states:

> It's a lot easier being a lesbian cop than being a gay cop. The occupation is dominated by heterosexual males. There's this bizarre idea that a woman that's a lesbian is somehow one of the guys. A gay officer is more of a threat to the whole macho mystique. The women in my department are much more open than the guys.[56]

Agreeing with Frazier is openly lesbian Paget Mitchell of the San Francisco Police Department. "Gay men always have it worse," Mitchell states. "My [male police] partners love the fact that I'm gay. They can now talk about their girlfriends with you. They think women are women and gay women are cops."[57]

Today, there appears to be more tolerance (or at least less overt hostility) from many citizens toward both lesbians and gay men. For example, the Association of Chief Police Officers in Britain has issued guidance aimed at eliminating discrimination. It states that "an individual's sexual orientation will be irrelevant to their gaining a job or promotion."[58] However, many individuals, not just in law enforcement but in all careers, still are hesitant to declare their sexual orientation. As one U.S. Deputy Police Chief stated to the authors, "I follow the military rule of 'Don't ask, don't tell.' I think it's better to be safe than sorry."

On the plus side, many departments today indicate that they have implemented a "zero tolerance" policy to try to eliminate any type of discrimination. Of course, most agencies would admit that it is impossible to totally eradicate this problem. However, there are a number of organizations designed to give support to gay and lesbian officers, including Florida LEGAL, which stands for Law Enforcement Gays and Lesbians; Gay Police Officers Action League of DC (GOAL-DC); and Gay and Lesbian Police Officers Advisory Committee (Denver).[59]

PERSONAL ISSUES

Although many of the women in law enforcement indicated that their families had supported them in their choice of careers, those who were married or living with a significant other faced various family problems. Today, in order to try to maintain middle-class status, both the adult male and the adult female in a household must be employed. Unfortunately, policing is not always a nine-to-five day job for either sex. Those on patrol may be required to work changing shifts, which means in the case of the female officer that when she is at home, her husband or male companion is not. If there are children in the relationship, child care becomes a major issue.

Finding someone to care for children (particularly if the officer is a single parent, if both partners work, or if both partners work the midnight to 5 A.M. shift) is extremely difficult if not impossible. Most police agencies do not take this issue into consideration. The one exception may be the Portland, Oregon, Police Bureau, "which offers on-site child care at the headquarters building as well as a drop-in child care facility near the courthouse."[60] This issue of adequate child care often determines whether a woman will be able to continue a career in law enforcement.

Another problem is the one that affects all women employed outside the home—who will end up doing the larger portion of the household tasks? Although many males tend to share a part of the housework, women do more than their share regardless of comparable hours of work. In the 1980s, sociologist Arlie Hochschild coined the term "second shift" to label this part of the employed woman's dual burden. About 30 percent of employed women fall into the category of "drudge wives," who hold full-time jobs and also do more than 60 percent of household work, excluding child care.[61]

In addition to the household chores of cleaning, laundry, cooking, and food shopping, women still tend to do the larger share of parenting in the home, particularly if the children are young. Of course, males in two-paycheck families (where the female may be engaged in shift work or does not work days) may have to become responsible for some child care while the mother is at work or at least make sure the children get to and from day care. If the couple's earnings are high enough, they may be able to afford an in-home caregiver who can relieve both parties of some child care and household chores. Still, in the 1990s, the average cost to the family for child care would have been $94 a week, with in-home caregivers receiving over $250 a week in some of the large metropolitan areas. For most dual earners, this cost is prohibitive; in addition, there tends to be a high turnover rate among individuals hired to care for children.[62]

Another issue mentioned by several women interviewed, and which can be a problem for both men and women, is that many times they are unable to share their work experiences with civilian family members or friends: One way women may reduce work and family conflicts is through marriage to a fellow officer. These police women may get stronger support for their work from those who understand their commitment to the job.[63] Without support and understanding, females may become isolated from spouses who work outside the law enforcement field. Other members of the police community tend to become their "family," and their close friends are other officers who understand and share the stress of the job.

STRESS

Stress is a major problem for police officers, as it is for people in general. However, police stress is not always obvious. It is not always the acute stress that can come from a post-shooting trauma. It can be obscure but debilitating, chronic stress that comes from continually seeing human misery and that may numb people's sensitivity to the problems and pain of others.[64]

As Kevin M. Gilmartin, author of *Emotional Survival for Law Enforcement*, indicated at the Rocky Mountain Women in Law Enforcement Conference, police are not called because things are right. They are never dispatched to a normal family dinner or where honesty is taking place. They deal with the "maddest, baddest and saddest" citizens. Cynicism and distrust of human nature may result, all of which adds to the stress of the job.[65]

In a speech on the effects of stress on police officers presented by

Dr. Dan Goldfarb to a group of union delegates, Goldfarb also indicated that police work was one of the top-ranked professions for job stress. He listed the biggest stressors as:

Killing someone in the line of duty
Having a partner killed in the line of duty
Lack of support by the department/bosses
Shiftwork and disruption of family time/family rituals
Daily grind of dealing with the lack of understanding of the public[66]

Although Goldfarb does not include it in his speech as a factor, lack of acceptance by male peers can add considerable stress to the lives of female personnel.

Stress that is not relieved may cause people to regress, to become more immature in their thinking and actions. Chronic stress may also numb an individual's sensitivity to others. Officers who encounter human harm and death day by day over months and years may become numb to human misery.[67] Gilmartin provides several ways to aid an individual in overcoming stress and becoming an "emotional survivor": practice aggressive personal time management and goal setting; practice physical fitness; control financial well-being and get out of the stress-related consumerism cycle; be aware of the multiple roles in one's life; see yourself as a survivor, not a victim.[68] If chronic stressors can be identified, police departments can take proactive steps, such as counseling, to help forestall officers' burnout, divorce, or suicide.

Because of the stress involved with the dangers of police work and the disruption of family time, divorce rates are high for those involved in policing. Holidays, weddings, and planned outings or vacations may have to take a backseat to the sudden, often unscheduled, demands of the job. While partners of the officers try to understand these interruptions, eventually the understanding ceases, and divorce may becoming the only recognized solution to the perceived problems.

Accurate statistics on the quantity and frequency of divorce for those in policing are difficult to ascertain. Retired Police Chief Chuck Pratt, author of *Police Headquarters*, writes that an informal survey of the men and women with whom he served indicated that

80 percent were divorced within three years of being hired. He found that within a twenty- to twenty-five-year career span, some officers would be married six to eight times. He did indicate that when both spouses were police officers, they had a great deal more in common than when only one of the individuals was an officer.[69] Although Pratt noted that a big factor in the high divorce rate was infidelity, he also stressed the need for communication between spouses about the requirements and the problems associated with the job.

SUICIDE

Novels and films often portray an aging, retired policeman without the support of his fellow officers or one who has seen too much of the seamy side of life "eating his gun." Stress in the job is also given as a reason for suicides of police officers, although this reason would apply to any number of other professions. Still, when an individual in the field of law enforcement commits suicide, it seems to be particularly newsworthy.

Suicide of a female officer is especially likely to make headlines, as was the case in 1997 of Barbara Ann Mahalak, 1 of only 9 women on the 239-member Detroit police force, who shot herself in the head the day after Thanksgiving. Although no suicide note was left, the newspaper indicated that "a simple case of the holiday blues" may have been the reason for the act. The article also notes that "female suicide by firearm is not as common as that of male police suicides,"[70] which may give the public the idea that police officers, in general, have high suicide rates.

In addition, an oft-cited 1995 Fraternal Order of Police study suggests that the suicide rate for law enforcement personnel is high—22 deaths per 100,000 compared with 12 deaths per 100,000 in the general population. Newspaper articles also cite "experts" who indicate that the suicide rate for police is at least twice that of the rest of the population.[71] However, a study from the New York Weill Cornell Medical Center, published in 2002, indicated that the rate of suicide for police officers was 14.9 per 100,000 persons compared to 18.3 per 100,000 for other New York City residents and concluded that officers "are less likely to commit suicide than the average New York City citizen." The study did find, however, that female officers had a higher risk of suicide than female residents, but the number of female police suicides was statistically small, indicating that further study would be needed.[72]

Many of the statistics cited do not take into consideration the race, gender, and age of people in the law enforcement field who commit suicide. Police officer suicide rates are almost always those of white males, as the national force is chiefly comprised of this race and gender. According to the *Sourcebook of Criminal Justice Statistics*, in 1997 approximately 72 percent of law enforcement personnel were white males, 11 percent were white or nonwhite females, and 17 percent were nonwhite males. The rate for white males age 25 to 55 must be considered, as this is the age group in which most of the suicides would be found. Taking the above information into consideration, Michael G. Aamodt and Nicole A. Stalnaker from Radford University in Virginia conclude that the rate of suicide for police officers "is not higher than would be expected for people of similar age, race, and gender. Thus any difference between law enforcement rates and rates in the general population can be completely explained by the race, gender, and age of people who enter the law enforcement field."[73]

Of course, losing even one individual through suicide is unacceptable to police departments, and some are taking steps to prevent suicides. The NYPD, together with its police union, has sponsored counseling programs for its personnel. However, some officers are leery of the programs as they feel that psychiatric evaluation may result in job sanctions of some kind.[74] There is still today in the minds of some people stigma connected with seeking counseling, and officers may fear being reassigned or missing out on promotions.

Although this chapter has pointed out the many problems women in policing face, it must again be emphasized that changes have been made. However, even with laws providing for equality in policing, gender-related incidents arise. A second-year Detective interviewed in July 2004 was quite irrate about recent treatment from her superior:

> Just a month ago I was assigned a case, and we had located a couple of suspects. Then my boss called me in and said, "I think it would be

> better if a male officer did the interviews. Since the suspects are tough males, they may not be willing to talk to a female." What was I to think? What was being said was that I was not really a police officer, that I couldn't cut it. Apparently, he feels that women officers can't handle a police job, something like just handling an interview. I guess what he wants me to do is only interview weak female suspects.

As this woman and many others pointed out, even when they think their departments have moved past what some call "discrimination nonsense," it is still there—sometimes when they least expect it.

CHAPTER 4

Climbing through the Ranks

> Something that happens to a woman that doesn't happen with men. . . . If a man gets promoted to sergeant . . . and he's put in charge of a squad of people on a shift, they're gonna kind of watch him for a while and he's gonna have to prove himself. . . . Put a woman in the same position? She's gonna have to prove it and prove it and prove it and prove it. You never stop having to prove yourself. Never!
>
> —Susan Ehrlich Martin, *Breaking and Entering,* 1995

Certainly, promotion for a female is possible; no one would deny that fact; and many seek promotion although it usually is a slow process and takes on average twenty to twenty-five years to achieve some of the top ranks. According to a 1998 survey by the International Association of Chiefs of Police, 69 percent of all women officers actively pursue promotions. The larger departments and those that actively recruit women see a larger number of females attempting to move up the ladder. However, gains by women are usually concentrated in the lowest tier of sworn police positions, with women holding 9.6 percent of supervisory posts but only 7.5 percent of top command jobs.[1] Since few reach the pinnacle in their profession, some of the reasons for this discrepancy need to be considered.

It should be pointed out that departments vary in their hierarchies and, therefore, in the number of positions available for upward mobility. State patrol agencies closely follow military ranks: Troopers, Corporals, Sergeants, and so on. Some sheriffs' departments consist of Patrol Officers, Sergeants, and Commanders. Police departments vary in that some have more tiers than others; some include the ranks of Corporal and Lieutenant while others do not. The fewer the command positions, the fewer the chances for mobility.

As in most bureaucracies, conflict among officers often occurs due to competition for the limited number of jobs. Some officers feel this undermines the view that the department is a tight-knit group. As one male officer stated, "We don't have a department of brethren. We have a department of individuals here."[2] Whether this is true or not of all departments, in general, women in law enforcement who seek promotion to higher levels continue to fight an uphill battle as they attempt to break through the glass ceiling, or "brass ceiling" as some in policing call it.

OPPORTUNITIES AND REACTIONS

Viewpoints on promotion chances differ, of course. According to an International Association of Chiefs of Police survey, more than half the male Police Chiefs in the survey stated that it *was not difficult* for women to gain promotion, while 34 percent stated that it *was difficult* to promote women. The Chiefs indicated that the primary reason for women not being promoted was the small number of women in the ranks for them to promote—only 18 percent. Another reason given was gender bias (9 percent), and this factor still has a large effect on female promotions despite efforts to stamp it out. As one female officer stated:

> Every time I've gone up in rank, I've gotten a jealous reaction from some men. Every time. And I really thought that would go away. . . . When I made lieutenant, before we got the list back as to who was where in rank order one of the guys came up to me and said, "Wherever you are in the list, I just hope that I'm one in front of you." And I said, "Why?" And he said, "'Cause you know they're not gonna pass

up an opportunity to promote a woman. And they have to get to me to get to you." Little comments like that.[3]

Another married female who did win a promotion to Deputy Chief in what she believed was a fair and equal process still heard negative comments from her male counterparts. Apparently they did not think she deserved the promotion and had received it simply because she was a female.

> I kind of laughed at them most of the time. I just told them, I said, "You know, there is always a reason why somebody gets promoted and somebody doesn't. You're either the bowling buddy of the Chief or you're Catholic or you golf with them or you're best friends or you're a woman or you're a minority." I said, "The reality is, I have earned all of my positions."[4]

Still, women and minorities may pass up opportunities to be promoted to supervisory positions if they believe they will face resistance or discrimination within their departments. Procedures for promotion vary, with many departments utilizing the "rule of three." This means that the top three scores on a promotional examination are given to a Chief of Police, who can select any one of these three for promotion. Obviously, this can cause dissension in the ranks, with both men and women, if a Chief chooses the individual with the third-place score over those in the upper two positions.

Some females indicated that bias was possible when this system was used. For example, in using the rule of three, if only one person needs to be hired, then the fourth person on the list is moved into the top three. As openings become available, the Chief can again select any of these top three, including the person who has just moved into position three. During this process there is always potential for bias. As one officer vying for Sergeant commented, "The chief can select anybody from the top three. If he didn't like you, you could sit on the promotion list as number one and still not get promoted. All he has to do is pick one of the three. It doesn't have to be number one. You may never make it, but it would seem unfair to possibly score the top on the test and never get picked."[5]

A Master Officer from Colorado, working in a department with one woman in a command position, wrote in a questionnaire that she thought she had been treated unfairly in the testing process just as she reached a top position in testing scores and should have been eligible for promotion.

> The first time I was pushed into testing by a Captain. I only had three years experience and had no desire to be a sergeant. . . . I was ranked eighth or ninth. The last time I tested I placed fifth; four were promoted, leaving me top of the list. The list was extended once, but the department let it expire at the end of December, knowing there would be two openings in April. I haven't and won't test again. The message has come through loud and clear.[6]

A police woman from Missouri wrote that in her department "two of six females had continually applied for promotions and had been denied." She indicated that there seemed to be "an effort to intentionally disqualify women from certain male dominated units of the police department."[7]

> I tested for them just like you guys have. I went through the same testing procedures, and I deserve as much as you did, and I am not going to change your mind. If you don't think I can do the job, show me how I can't do it, [but] at least give me a chance to show you that I can.[8]

Chief Nan Hegerty indicated that she always tried to make her reaction a positive one when she heard negative comments or felt resentment from male office colleagues. "I found I couldn't change what people think," she explained in a *USA Today* interview. "The only thing I could do was stay the course and keep my eye on the job."[9]

Captain Michele Miuccio, who is one of only three females Captains in the history of the Boca Raton, Florida, Police Department, thought that the attitude of some male officers toward female officers had been altered to a degree as some of them had been raised by a single female parent or in a family in which the mother was dominant. Quoted in the *Boca Raton News,* Miuccio stated she felt that if the Police Chief was "accepting of whoever you are, it rolls down. I'm hoping that women will see, especially in this agency, that they can and will be promoted to supervisory positions based on their skills, not their gender." Although her comments were more positive, she did indicate that female officers still face greater obstacles in the law enforcement profession.

MORE PROBLEMS

Practically all police departments evaluate their personnel, male and female, on an annual or semiannual basis. Performance evaluations can have a major impact on what assignments employees are given, whether they get special training, and whether or not individuals move up the career ladder. The military, which is similar in structure to a police department, rewards more highly those individuals who have been in combat. Most military women never see combat, and this is reflected on their evaluations, making it harder for them to be promoted to upper ranks. Like the military, police departments have assignments that are more desired and more valuable—those that require considerable physical strength or are considered more dangerous. Women often get assignments still considered better handled by females, such as domestic violence units or child abuse investigations, while men are chosen for motorcycle patrols, undercover narcotics units, or Special Weapons and Tactics (SWAT) teams. Getting assigned to many different jobs helps both males and females seeking to be promoted. Being denied some of the more promotable jobs negatively affects women's opportunities for advancement, as they are not viewed as having proved themselves worthy to move to higher positions.

Harrington and Lonsway cite some female officers who feel that a double standard exists in judging the performance of females versus males regardless of the assignments. These women feel that they are constantly judged more harshly than their male counterparts and have to outperform the males in order to be considered on the same level. They believe that they have to "make more arrests, recover more stolen automobiles, or write more traffic tickets to receive the same 'competent' rating as a male peer."[10]

When women are promoted to ranks with more authority, many male officers continue to view them as interlopers and feel that the female officers may have been given unfair advantage in the competition process. The women may have to prove themselves before being accepted in the supervisory position. Sheriff Sergeant Lisa Grosskrueger succinctly states the problem facing many females: "Nineteen years of experience and I *still* have to prove myself."[11] This does not mean that Grosskrueger wishes to remain at her present rank. She indicates that she plans to be promoted to Lieutenant in 2005 and to Captain in 2010.

Another woman supervisor recalls finally being told that she had won acceptance from her male peers. "[The unit was] in a situation in the town where one of the officers was assaulted and the offender's run off and I chased three and arrested three on foot . . . then the shift were completely different towards me, it was like, 'Yeah, you've proved yourself now, that you're . . . one of the boys, you can get involved.' "[12]

Chief Ella Bully-Cummings explained that she gradually won a grudging acceptance from many of her male colleagues. However, she, too, felt that women were "held to a higher standard. We have to be extraordinary."[13] For some females who have worked long and hard to simply prove themselves as officers the idea of having to do it all over again to achieve a supervisory role may serve to lower their aspirations.

Another problem reported by several police women is being addressed continually with familiarities such as "honey," "dear," or "love" by their male counterparts, which, although possibly not intended to do so, could demean their position as a supervisor. As Myra L. explained,

> Frequently, I've had my fellow [male] officers call me "dear" or "honey." Actually most times it's "hon," and they do this in formal situations like when I'm with some person I've just arrested or trying to talk with a witness or when they tell me I've got a phone call waiting. It's certainly not appropriate, and it's very demeaning. Also, how can I expect these same men to take me seriously [as their boss] if or when I'm promoted. To them, I'm not good enough material to be a supervisor. I'm just "hon."

A continuing issue facing police women as they move up the ladder, especially as they are required to take on more challenging supervisory positions, is the difficulty encountered in balancing the different components of family life and career. They may have trouble fulfilling necessary family obligations, and many female officers see neglecting their family as too high a price to pay for advancement.

Carrying their weight on the job and finding the time necessary to study for police exams required for promotion also may become overwhelming for both male and female officers. However, several police women interviewed felt that the burden on females was greater than that on males because of the "second shift" women take on in the home.

One Deputy Police Chief, a twenty-five-year-veteran, lamented the lack of time necessary to study for her various promotion tests and felt there simply had not been enough hours in the day to take care of all of her work and home obligations. In her own experience, as she moved through the ranks, she could only "hit the books" after everyone else in the family was in bed:

> It's not uncommon at our agency for someone who really wants to get promoted to take a month or more off to study prior to a test. Others use their evenings or weekends for studying. I probably could have passed some tests a lot higher and a lot sooner if, like most of the guys, I had a wife at home to take care of me—you know, to fix the meals, take care of the kids. I could take time off, but I could not just sit for hours a day and study like some of my male counterparts could. . . . I had crying babies; it made a whole lot of difference because I couldn't ignore those crying babies whereas I think sometimes a man can do that and let somebody else take care of them. Society just places requirements on women that they don't place on men.[14]

Also, if going back to school for a university degree to help with promotion is added to the equation, life becomes even more complicated. In an interview, one woman appeared to be amazed that she had attempted to improve her job level. "I began to go to college full time. I worked eleven to seven at night, and I went to college classes on Tuesdays and Thursdays during the day, Wednesday nights from six to ten and Saturday from eight to four. I would never do that again and work full time, divorced with three kids! It is amazing that I could find my way home."[15]

Although these problems may not be unique to law enforcement, women in policing repeatedly emphasized how difficult it was to give the appropriate attention to all the elements of their lives. Recalling her hectic schedule as she successfully moved up in rank, an officer laughingly stated, "I haven't slept in eighteen years."

For the female in law enforcement these complications mean that she may have to forgo or delay seeking promotions in order to accommodate both family and a career. Being promoted to a higher rank does not guarantee that officers will be able to have a desk job or to leave shift work. A female supervisor emphasized that women need to be aware of the complications that may arise:

> I see a lot of women at some point in their careers decide that it is more important to raise their families. That's fine. There is no problem there. But when you set your sight on getting to a certain level . . . you sometimes can't do both, no doubt about it. . . . I know a lot of women I have talked to, and they don't want to give up Christmas at home, they don't want to give up evenings with their children. . . . But they have to realize when they come into this career that there [are] going to be sacrifices.[16]

This supervisor also explained that the female officers needed to discuss the job with their family members and get them involved in their decisions to try to be promoted. "I think there is too much of the romance about the career and not enough about the full aspects of it—you know, long tedious nights in the cold and the rain, people spit on you, throwing up on you—that and the impact on your family. . . . It is a difficult job and everyone needs to understand that."[17] Promotion does not mean that an individual will move to a five-day workweek or not have to leave a desk job and go back on patrol.

A HELPING HAND

A further issue, which many women are reluctant to discuss, is nonsupportive females in law enforcement—what some women call their "worst enemy"—who try to block a woman's promotion or at least fail to mentor her as she attempts to secure a higher position. Men have made use of informal mentoring for years through what is called "the good old boys' network." On occasion women at the top will support other female executives but go to great lengths to separate themselves from those of lower rank.

Brown and Heidensohn provide some interesting personal stories of police women who were disillusioned with the concept of sisterhood or mentoring. "Women can be quite bitchy," one bluntly stated. Another felt that women did not go out of their way to be helpful to those seeking advancement.[18]

Also, many police women indicated that they were surprised at encountering a great deal of jealousy from their female peers when they were promoted. One woman stated that she "had expected some resentment from the men, but I never felt that the other women would turn on me." Another woman, a Deputy Chief, expressed similar feelings:

> Once I promoted, the women I'd considered my peers and allies on the force became very distant. On the surface they expressed their approval of my promotion and even would congratulate me. But later I heard comments to the effect that they thought I had somehow manipulated my promotion. They really were jealous of my moving up and leaving them behind.[19]

Similar comments were made in Brown and Heindesohn's study. One police woman indicated that her female colleagues were very envious of her being able to advance in rank and were angry with her. Another mentioned that a close colleague was "difficult in that she does not wish to see anyone succeed around her . . . she doesn't encourage you . . . she speaks down . . . she distances herself."[20]

As she was promoted through the ranks, still another woman

expressed her shock at the attitudes of other officers she had considered to be close friends:

> Nobody hardly talked to me for two weeks after my promotion to Sergeant. I thought to myself, "Whoa! What's going on here?" People that were really my friends dealt with it better, but even from them it wasn't the great congratulations that one expects for that level of promotion. I was rather hurt by this reaction. After all, I had worked hard for the upgrade, and I thought the others, particularly the women, would be happy for me. But they resented me.[21]

Even women who have made it to top-ranking positions and who have mentored other women may do so only until their career path is perceived to be in jeopardy. A Deputy Police Chief explained the internal conflict she faced regarding mentoring as she moved through the ranks:

> I always thought that I was "pro" women. When I began my career in law enforcement, I was mentored by a male Lieutenant who retired at that rank. When I tested for the Captain's position and made it, he was my biggest fan. Because of his support, I felt it was so important to mentor others that I became an advocate of mentoring. However, when a female sergeant I had mentored from early on was testing for the position of Lieutenant, I started to get nervous. I felt she had her sights on Chief of Police, just like I did. I could see that she might eventually be a threat to me as there are so few positions for promotion past lieutenant. I couldn't believe my attitude, but there it was. I really hate to confess to these feelings. It was a real internal conflict. Do I help her promote—possibly past me. Or do I stop the mentoring process?

On the other hand, there are those who receive accolades for their mentoring. Some women expressed the feeling that they had been successful in being promoted only because of the mentoring they had received in their departments:

> I have had mentors all along the way. I have had people that have been willing to help me learn and grow and also helped me find

> experiences that readied me for the next level. And in most cases those have been supervisors . . . sergeants who helped me get ready for that detective position or my lieutenant who said, "You need to go for this." My readiness for chief really came from mentoring and career development opportunities. Some I sought; some I was given by my chief who was my mentor.[22]

A Lieutenant of Detectives in New Jersey considered her first Chief to be her most significant mentor. However, she "also had several other male officers who I have looked up to and learned from" and indicated that she "mentored those officers, both male and female, who have reached out for my help." An investigator from Colorado stated that she had "been encouraged to test [for promotion] by my current sergeant, lieutenant, fellow officers and other supervisors within the department."

Sheriff Margo Frasier also indicated that she acted as a mentor for both women and men and felt she had an obligation to do so. She didn't get promoted on her own, she knew: "I got here because I had people who cared about me, helped me, supported me. . . . I owe that back."[23]

Of course, many times, as Sergeant Lisa Grosskrueger, a nine-year veteran, lamented, "There are simply no females on the command staff to act as mentors."[24] In that case, women must look to male personnel for advice on moving up the ladder. However, both male and female officers already on the force often are unwilling to mentor or do not seem to recognize the importance of becoming mentors to those who might later become competitors for scarce top positions.

DOESN'T EVERYONE WANT TO BE PROMOTED?

To be fair, women may not wish to be promoted from a position in which they have become comfortable. For instance, some like to be on patrol. Others may have found a position as a Detective or in the Identification Bureau; some may be employed as a school resource officer and have become accustomed to a daytime shift where they only have to be on call during school hours and have weekends free. Many women (and men) do not wish to vie for a supervisory role and are content with their present status. With promotion, they may have little choice of assignments and be required to return to a graveyard shift, be back on street patrol, or end up in what some consider a boring desk job. Officer Jean Marie Bready presents a good example of the dilemma sometimes faced when considering promotion.

> At this time I have no desires to advance to lieutenant or above. I very much enjoy actively working the streets, hands on police work, etc. I am currently assigned to a desk position in Personnel and Training and am having a hard time not being on the road. Maybe later in my career I will gain an appreciation for command work.[25]

Asked if she were considering promotion, Officer Kristin Touchstone indicated, "At this point, no. I'm still trying to grasp the job of patrol officer and am not able to fathom supervising anyone."[26] She also indicated that there were no women in command in her department as she is its only female officer.

The size of a department may also be a factor when individuals are considering whether or not to work for promotion. New Jersey Police Captain Margaret T. indicated that she would like to advance to the rank of Deputy Chief but was not certain that she wanted to manage a police department, "at least one this size. Possibly a smaller department or at a university."

New Jersey Police Lieutenant Barbara Steinberg was very definite about her promotion aspirations. When queried as to whether she wished to advance to the position of Chief of Police, she answered, "Of course I do. I do not want the others [women] to feel that we have a glass ceiling."[27]

Sometimes officers may wish to be promoted to a particular level but no further. A Lieutenant in an Arizona Police Department disclosed that she would like to be promoted to Commander "but no higher." She also mentioned that in that agency of 2,900 personnel, there were only two female Commanders out of twenty-seven.[28]

Patrol Officer Suzette Freidenberger stated that although she had not been promoted so far, she hoped to be promoted during the course of her career. "At this point in my career," she wrote in a questionnaire, "I would only want to promote as far as Sergeant. But that may change later in life."[29]

One officer decided to go back to school, which led her into the administration of her police agency. "I went back to college to get my master's. . . . You know, you got back to talking to people who appreciated what police do and the bigger picture. . . . I decided that I wanted to get involved in the administration of the police department."[30]

Lieutenant Deborah Cady, in a South Dakota Police Department, indicated that she would consider the possibility of testing for the rank of Captain. "I have not had any difficulties with the promotion process," Cady wrote. "Command staff has encouraged me to take part in promotions."[31]

Unlike Cady, however, most of the female officers responding about promotion (those interviewed or those who completed questionnaires) felt that promotions for women generally were difficult to achieve. They encouraged women to try to be promoted to supervisory positions but felt that the male-dominated career field still tended to disqualify females. In fact, one respondent to the authors' questionnaire, who asked that neither she nor her agency be identified, explained that she was hesitant to respond in writing.

> I have filed an EEOC for discrimination in promotion . . . to the rank of Captain. . . . Our agency has never had a female law enforcement captain. . . . I am the third woman to file a promotional EEOC complaint in our agency in the last 3 years. . . . EEOC found cause in my claim and has referred it to the Dept. of Justice."

This woman indicated that she had been in law enforcement for twenty-three years, had exceptional performance evaluations, no disciplinary problems, and diverse agency experience. She was disappointed that more women were not reaching higher positions. Without women in higher ranks, she wondered, "Where are the role models for us women?"

Still, many women have not been deterred by overt or subtle discrimination, hostility from coworkers, or family problems and either have been promoted or were contemplating moving to higher ranks. Some, as the following chapter shows, will make it to the top in their agencies.

CHAPTER 5

▼

Reaching the Pinnacle

> Girls live in a "flat" social structure. They play games in which power is shared equally. There is never a captain doll player of a winner in a game of nurse. Girls who try to order others around or push ahead of their playmates are usually called bossy and have few friends.
>
> —Heim and Golant, *Smashing the Glass Ceiling*, 1995

"I never forget, and I'm a little bitter. I went through a competition for Police Chief two years ago. What an experience!" exclaimed one Deputy Chief. "During the competition, officers were quoted in the newspapers as saying that they would lose esteem in the eyes of other law enforcement officers if they had a female chief. And you know I'm thinking, 'Good grief, this is almost the 21st century. Grow up, guys!' Obviously, I didn't get the job."[1]

Of course, promotion to a high position such as Chief of Police for a female is occurring in the twenty-first century. However, one of the major issues for most women in police work continues to be the lack of promotional opportunity to the top ranks. While the popular television series *Law and Order* has had a female managing one of its divisions and aggressively directing male Detectives, this portrayal is only now beginning to depict reality. Statistics show that few women have moved beyond the lower levels of management. In his article "The Past, Present, and Future of Women in Policing," Sean A. Grennan cites a 1983 study that indicated the disproportionate number of females in supervisory positions within 106 police agencies across the United States. Several of the larger departments (in Miami; Long Beach, California; St. Paul, Minnesota; Dallas, Texas; and Newark, New Jersey) had no women in top command, while some large police departments, such as those in Chicago, Boston, and New York City, indicated numbers from 3 to 5 percent.[2]

This trend continues, as Margaret Moore, Director of the National Center for Women & Policing, pointed out in 2002: "Not only is there a smaller percentage of women in policing, but women are virtually absent at the highest ranks of law enforcement, holding only 7.3% of top command positions. In fact, more than half (55.9%) of large agencies surveyed report no women in top command."[3]

A 2002 Feminist Majority Foundation press release cited a survey done in conjunction with the Justice and Safety Center of Eastern Kentucky University that studied small U.S. police departments. The survey showed that of 384 smaller and rural law enforcement agencies surveyed (those with fewer than 100 sworn personnel), in only 3.4 percent do females hold top command jobs. Of the smaller departments, 87.4 percent had no women in top command positions.[4]

According to Grennan, there may be an actual conspiracy on the part of male police executives to utilize certain strategies to obstruct the upward mobility of high-profile females. He cites as an example the NYPD: "It seems that NYPD administrators find it beneficial to their egos to remove highly successful female police executives from high-profile positions and put them in low-profile assignments somewhere in headquarters. This reassignment will, ultimately, force this officer to retire because she knows that once this takes place, there is no opportunity for upward mobility and promotion."[5]

Although some females have moved into high-level positions since Grennan's and Moore's statistics were published, they are still underrepresented in proportion to the number of women in law enforcement. Part of the difficulty for women lies in the police management hierarchy. It is rigid and very narrow at the top, with only a limited number of middle management and administration positions available for either males or females. This pyramid structure and the emphasis that having a good arrest record is the best means to promotion perpetuate the attitudes about policing being a man's job.[6]

The process for becoming Police Chief of a municipal police department is completely different from testing within a department for the positions of Sergeant or Captain. Individuals interested in applying for the lower positions must apply to the city government and usually face oral boards made up of private citizens, interviews by officials in city management, and, sometimes, many hours of written tests. The Chief of Police position is selected by people *outside* the department who usually have little knowledge of the candidate's past performance or managerial ability. As is shown later in this chapter, the process is often very political and involves "who one knows" not "what is known." (In most cases, the position of Deputy Chief is appointed by the Police Chief in the department.)

Generally, women in law enforcement who seek promotion to higher levels continue to fight an uphill battle. While conditions for females in all police departments have improved over the last two decades, many hurdles still exist and must be acknowledged and dealt with if a female wishes to remain or advance in her chosen field. Mentoring (see Chapter 4) continues to be an important asset for those trying to reach the pinnacle.

One female chief feels that it is the duty of leaders to provide as much encouragement as possible to those who come behind. She has mentored both men and women to successfully reach the position of Chief:

> I think we have a duty to do that—men or women—it doesn't matter. I think we have a duty as leaders to mentor, and I feel proud and successful when people under my command are promoted. I have always felt that. In fact, I have a whole little cadre of my own that I have helped groom to be police chiefs. And that makes me proud.[7]

Sometimes mentoring from another female is not always possible, however, as there may be no other women in the department or the women in the department may not be in a position to mentor. One woman stated that while she had been mentored by several individuals as she worked through various levels of promotion, "obviously none of my mentors were female because there was no female who outranked me. My mentors were always men."

Also, even though she strongly believes in the necessity for mentoring, one Deputy Police Chief explains that in her new role as an administrator, her ability to mentor has been considerably altered. As simply another member of the force, she could share in the gossip and gripes. Her new position no longer provides this same latitude for camaraderie.

> I think I did a lot more mentoring when I was a sergeant than I have since becoming part of the administration. That's because there are some things that you just can't tell me, that, as part of the administration, I just can't simply listen to. If you tell me certain things, I have to do something about them. For example, if you tell me there is sexual harassment, things like that, I can't simply advise. I have to take action, and so that's cut down on some of the women coming to me as they used to. We can't simply share our problems as we used to. I feel very strongly that we have to mentor each other, but my new position sometimes puts me in a very awkward position. . . . I'm not sure I mentor much any more.[8]

It is not only a good idea for women to know mentors in their departments; they need to make contact or network with Deputy Chiefs or Chiefs in other cities and states.

NETWORKING

For women who seek to reach top positions, networking skills may be as important as (if not more important than) mentoring, especially if their goal is position of Police Chief. Networking has not been one of most women's strong points. However, becoming a public figure in the community with some name recognition is almost a necessity. This can be accomplished by joining civic organizations such as Kiwanis and Rotary, giving presentations to various community groups, and providing information to the media as the department's Public Relations officer. Those individuals encountered outside law enforcement may be the ones an applicant will face on a search or screening committee. Networking with other Chiefs of Police or Deputy Chiefs throughout the country (male or female) may also aid the individual in attaining her ultimate goal.

One Chief attended conferences of police women and stated that these helped her network with others so that in the top position she felt less isolated. The conferences were "my time to come together with other women because when . . . I was the only Commander you never have any peers. So this was . . . my Mecca to get rejuvenated and that meant you could fight for another year."[9]

"I do network at classes and conferences, but with just as many men as women," indicated Officer Jean Marie Bready. "When networking, I seek out people who are like minded or who have skills/knowledge that excite me."[10] Chief Lynne Johnson indicated that she has done networking "over my career and continue to do so. You get new and different perspectives while at the same time hear things that confirm that you aren't the only one who has experienced a lot of things."[11]

For her dissertation, author Sandra K. Wells interviewed a number of women who had sought promotion to Deputy Chief or Chief of Police. Their comments provide insight into their paths to the top. As one woman stated, her Chief pointed out the importance of networking if she were going to vie for the Police Chief position.

> My chief told me one of the reasons I made such a good deputy chief was because of my networking skills . . . and that I did understand the politics. I am a very big believer in networking and doing all the things required of networking. And I made that decision probably . . . when I was a lieutenant . . . that I needed to know people. . . . So I knew the city council people, I knew the people in budget . . . and I think this is what the secret agenda is. The women don't do their homework. Women are really terrible at networking. They do not take

> the time; they do not belong to associations; they don't take the time to attend meetings. . . . As a deputy chief, your job is to network. Your job is to go out there and sell the department.[12]

Still another woman interviewed explained the importance of networking, of becoming more visible to the public.

> Most police agencies have very few women within them, so I got involved with the state-wide police organization early on because there were so few of us [women]. But you really need to have some kind of networking support from various organizations even if they are composed mostly of males. And if there are some women's groups, they may get you in contact with other women who are having some of the same problems that you have. But, more importantly, it also gets you used to networking and lets you become known by many people.[13]

Of course, there could be a downside to becoming fairly well known by the public. As some officers point out, personal privacy seems to disappear. One Chief indicated that she did not realize how much she was watched in her community.

> I can't go any place in town without someone recognizing me—probably from newspaper photos. For example, just the other day I was having lunch with a consultant about a project the department is involved in. We must have been interrupted six times, just people coming over. They want to complain about something or just meet me. I feel edgy just ordering a drink—just a bad thing to do. Frankly, you have to leave the state and go on vacation to sit down and have a bottle of wine.[14]

Many high-ranking officers cannot help but chafe at the public scrutiny they receive. Some indicate that it limits their ability to work as they please and is similar to the treatment (both positive and negative) that those in all high-profile occupations receive. As one fifteen-year female veteran stated, "I don't like the microscope that we are kept under from both the public and the administration."[15]

FINALLY MAKING IT TO THE TOP

There are women—a few—who break through the "brass ceiling." They get to see their dreams realized as they succeed in attaining some of the top positions in law enforcement. Patricia Lamphere was promoted to Assistant Chief of the Seattle Field Support Bureau in 1992. She had joined the force in 1967 as a police woman in the old Policewomen's Bureau and was assigned to work in the juvenile division. Roberta Webber, who joined the Portland Police Bureau in 1971, was assigned to an area entitled the Women's Protective Division before transferring to the Drug and Vice Division and serving undercover for a period of time. She eventually made her way up the ranks to Deputy Chief of Operations and in 1994 to Deputy Chief.[16]

Lieutenant Colonel Suzanne G. Devlin was appointed by the Fairfax County supervisors to the position of Acting Chief. Replacing Chief J. Thomas Manger, Devlin became the first woman to lead Virginia's largest local police force. However, her rise to this position was not without controversy. In 1989, she sued the department, claiming she had been passed over for promotion to Lieutenant because of her gender, and won an out-of-court settlement. "You have to take a historical perspective," Devlin said in a 2004 *Washington Post* interview. "In the early years, that's the way it was. They were not ready for women to be here. . . . When I think of the way it was then and the way it is now, the environment is much more receptive to women."[17]

Devlin joins a handful of women who lead law enforcement agencies in the Washington, D.C., area, including Gaithersburg Police Chief Mary Ann Viverette, Arlington Sheriff Beth Arthur, and Metro Police Chief Polly Hansen. Although Devlin is Acting Chief, she will face competition for the permanent job from two other male Deputy Chiefs. "We expect all three [Deputy Chiefs] to be very competitive," stated Fairfax County Executive Anthony Griffin.[18]

Some police women in top positions even receive honors, as was the case with Assistant Chief Barbara Wong. The Hawaii Joint Police Association commended her for "her achievements in the face of competition" and indicated that her "performance is a role model for all the men and women in the Honolulu Police Department."[19]

Like the other women, Penny Harrington was successful in her bid to move to the top. In 1985 Harrington became the first woman Chief of Police of a major city in the United States—Portland, Oregon. By the time she resigned the position seventeen months later, she was in command of more than eight hundred police officers and administered a budget of $57 million. Still, her term as Chief was not without problems. Allegations were made that she was "soft on drugs" and had "defects of leadership." In spite of any problems she may have encountered, Harrington comments positively about reaching the top:

> Once you get up there . . . you have a major impact. You have the ability to make major changes in the way that agency operates. . . . The feeling of accomplishment that you get . . . is wonderful. But as you get higher in the ranks, and you are actually able to change the way policing is done in the community and change the way your department treats its employees, that's when you get the real satisfaction in knowing you have made a difference.[20]

However, Chief Penny Harrington states in a 2004 article that the number of those making it to the position of Police Chief in a major police agency, herself included, can be counted on one hand: Elizabeth Watson, Houston; Carol Mehrling, Montgomery County, Maryland; Jan Strauss, Mesa, Arizona.[21] Still, several sites on the Internet provide an extensive and more encouraging list of states across the country in which women are achieving top positions in law enforcement. These include California, Texas, Massachusetts, Connecticut, Wisconsin, Illinois, Virginia, Ohio, and New York.

A recent and interesting climb to the top was that of Julia Grimes, a Trooper for more than two decades, who in May 2003 was appointed Director of the Division of Alaska State Troopers. She is the first woman to hold that post and oversees 363 Troopers in more than thirty communities. Like Harrington, Grimes felt she could have "such a broad positive impact. [I can] take everything I've learned about being a trooper over the last 20 years and put it into practice to make the division better."[22]

However, the recent success of most of these women shouldn't make one assume that women are taking over the majority of top positions in law enforcement. According to the 1999 National Directory of Law Enforcement Administrators, there were more than thirteen thousand police departments in the United States, but the position of Chief of Police was held by *fewer than one hundred women*, or less than 1 percent. Fewer than twenty of these women represent cities with populations over 20,000, certainly not to be considered the major agencies referred to by Harrington. (Usually women who are Sheriffs or Deputy Sheriffs also are found in small towns. Many times they are elected to the top position of Sheriff simply because no male was interested in the job. The stereotype of the small-town female Sheriff was recently presented to the public in the popular movie *Fargo*.)

TRYING OUT

The search for Police Chief is often a nationwide search. The process for selection varies in police departments but usually includes oral boards, assessment centers, oral presentations, and sometimes written examinations. Often, because the position is a political selection made by the city's governing body, it ends in a political battle. Interviews with women who have applied for this sought-after position or who have been selected revealed their feelings about the process and the results. Two applicants explained their feelings about the politics involved in their quest for the top position.

> Well, it was a terribly bitter political battle. At that time, although it was the recommendation of the city manager, it took a confirmation vote of at least a majority of the city commissioners or council, whatever you want to call it. So there was heavy politicking by other candidates, and it was one of those dirty-type campaigns. Although I had a good reputation in the community and the support of the former chief, I was basically standing on my work ethic and my work record. The person that waged the heaviest campaign against me eventually became the union president of the command officers. So there was a big cooperative effort going on right there from the union guys to get him selected.

> At any rate we had a fairly new city manager and, as there was a vacancy for fire chief and police chief, he was going to form a committee to allow input. The committee included labor reps and [city] commissioners and so forth to help make recommendations for the selection, although it was the manager who had nominated the candidates for the positions. Well, the appointed committee became so embroiled in controversy and politicking that the city manager disbanded the committee, appointed me chief, resigned from his position and moved to another place.[23]

A Deputy Chief who did not end up with the coveted top position discussed the stress involved in her attempt. She had taken a psychological intelligence test which she indicated "consisted of all kinds of unbelievable questions. I couldn't see how they related to the job." The test was administered in a time-controlled environment where the candidates had to respond to a series of questions "about our history and the future of the police department."[24]

Then the candidates were questioned by a professional panel consisting of the district attorney, Sheriff, Police Chiefs from other jurisdictions, and academics involved in the criminal justice field. A second panel consisting of citizens from the community also met with the candidates. Finally, a decision was made, and the woman felt it was done to be politically correct. "It was a biased decision," she stated. "It was biased in that they felt they had to choose a racial or ethnic minority. That's what they did. I guess I just wasn't the right minority."[25]

Still another participant in the selection process commented at length on the use of citizens in the interview process and the fact that these citizens might not be knowledgeable about the necessary requirements for a particular police job:

> The city manager put together a citizens' committee of seven members, but they had no guidance from anybody in the city administration. The committee members made their own rules as far as what questions they would ask, how they would ask them and if there would be any follow up. There were six of us—three deputy chiefs, a captain and two sergeants trying for the position. Nobody ever explained to the committee members that you can't take a sergeant and

make him a chief in any agency of any size. They were of the understanding that if we were there, we could be chief. So they took a sergeant and eliminated a deputy chief and a captain from the running.

After it was all over, the city manager told me that he thought the race was between me and the person finally selected as chief. I asked him if the citizens' committee eliminating me made it easier for him to sleep at night. He could have made a choice himself but didn't. He never did answer my question, but having the citizens to blame gave him an easy out. He simply didn't want to take any heat for whatever decision he might have made.

I know the citizens' committees are a big trend in the country right now, and I certainly don't underestimate them. I think having citizen involvement in any process is important, but they need to be informed about what they're looking for, about diversity issues, the whole thing. Do you eliminate someone with a master's degree and five or six years of command experience for somebody who doesn't have it, who only has a four-year degree and no administrative experience? Can that person walk in and be a chief? Obviously, the city manager didn't think so, but he didn't bother to tell the committee that.[26]

Another interesting interview was that of a participant who mentioned some of her feelings of ambivalence when she tossed her hat in the ring for Police Chief:

After their nationwide search they had, I think, maybe 110 people that applied. . . . It was a pretty tough process. I mean, we had an assessment center, we had interviews, we had presentations before the mayor and city council, and we had a lot of psychological evaluations. It was a pretty long and drawn out process and pretty stressful. Also you have to think about what your friends in the department think about you applying for the position. You know you want to stay here and work. I mean, I definitely did not want to leave this department, so one way or another, if you get the job or not, you are going to be here. Everyone knows you are applying for the position. What if you don't get it, and that's a real possibility. I guess what I'm saying is

> I didn't want my simply applying to have ruined all of my relationships if I wasn't selected. I was afraid I'd be considered uppity by some for even applying. I wanted the job, but sometimes I wondered if I was doing the right thing by trying for it.[27]

However, this applicant could put her fears to rest. The position was eventually narrowed down to three applicants, and the female being interviewed was "lucky enough" to be selected for the position of Chief. As she had anticipated, in that new position, her relationships with former associates would necessarily change. Asked to comment on why she thought she had been the individual chosen, she gave a great deal of credit to a former boss.

> The chief that originally hired me . . . I know had done everything he could to position me correctly. He was a great mentor. He was a great endorser. . . . One of the things I will always be grateful to him for is that he made me do things I didn't want to do. I mean, he made me give lots of programs at various organizations and schools and, you know, join all the civic organizations. I also taught classes for a community college. Still, just as an example of how few female chiefs or deputy chiefs there are, as a deputy chief I went to a seminar recently. Apparently, the seminar coordinators were not prepared for a female. When I checked in my little "hostess gift," there was a pouch of Red Man's chewing tobacco. That kind of says it all! But you know they were nice guys. They were a little bit old fashioned, but the chief just made me kind of part of the scenery. So it became natural that I was there. It was not like, "Oh, look, it's a woman." It was more like, "She is here from a department that has a really outstanding reputation, not only in the state but in the entire region." So I just sort of blended in with the men.[28]

This individual was quick to add that, even though the Police Chief who had been her mentor was gone from the area and a new city administrator was in place, she felt like she . . . "would be lying if I didn't say I felt like I had an inside track . . . although I never felt like the process was a sham. I felt I was the best candidate."

As was mentioned in Chapter 1, like Police Chiefs, there are examples of female Sheriffs. Margo Frasier was not appointed to her top position in Travis County, Texas. She was elected in 1997 as that county's first female Sheriff. Travis County appears to be fairly gender-blind, for in 1998 36 percent of the top command positions and nearly 28 percent of the supervisory positions were held by women. Margo's opponent in the election was the male Chief Deputy, but she had the endorsement of the Officers' Association, which aided her in the campaign. "That just blew away the public in a lot of ways," she says, "because . . . I don't think that's what they expected from the good old boys—that they'd be endorsing a woman to be the sheriff."[29]

Of course, some women state that they did not join their respective police departments with aspirations of advancing to Police Chief, Sheriff, or head of the State Patrol. When they considered the possibility of vying for the top, the challenge seemed overwhelming. For example, one female officer watched the difficulties her Chief went through in the selection process and determined that she would not have a chance battling the political aspects. Therefore, she decided she would never even make the attempt.

> Our deputy chief (female) tried for chief and I said, "I'm not testing here right now 'cause we have gone through a political thing with our mayor, and he isn't going to promote any of us." And I told the mayor that. The number one and two positions were our people, and the female deputy chief, I think, was number nine. The mayor overlooked all of them and chose number three who was an outsider. It was because of this political crap we had gone through.[30]

Aside from politics and the possibility that testing and interviewing may be biased, other factors may have an impact on female promotions. Some women lack the seniority required to be eligible for higher-level positions, for, generally, an individual has to spend twenty to twenty-five years in a department to reach the top.[31] Some simply do not want to be promoted for personal reasons such as family responsibilities. Some women (and men) decide to stay in a particular niche—the identification area, a Detective position, the DARE program—that may provide a work schedule with fairly regular hours. Promotion to another position may require that the officer go back on the street in a patrol car, and, due to family commitments, the individual may not desire or feel able to fulfill this new assignment. Also, as one female pointed out, a woman may end up being placed in a certain area of policing for most of her career, which may not provide her with the experiences necessary to fill a top job. "Where male officers have moved around to positions in the department and have varied experiences, they are more prepared for promotion interviews. They haven't been as one-dimensional as the women."

It is also thought by some that a "masculine ethic" is associated with the ideology of the managerial idea (see Chapter 6). Such masculine qualities as a hard-line approach to problem solving, analytical planning abilities, and an intellectual rather than an emotional point of view when dealing with problem solving and decision making are thought to be necessary for those reaching top positions.[32] Certainly, all these qualities are needed but, unfortunately, are not thought to be part of the feminine personality. The ability to relate to and communicate with staff and the public should be of prime importance when considering candidates for the top spots.

Both female Deputy Chiefs and Chiefs stated that, although they felt they had an understanding of what the position entailed, they were not always prepared for the required decision making. Of course, each leader will face different requirements, and it is possible that unless they actually reach the pinnacle of Chief, they cannot fully recognize the challenges to be faced. For the Chief (as President Harry Truman stated), "The buck stops here!" The female Chief will discover that the unilateral decisions, many centered on tough personnel issues, will be hers alone. One Chief explained in almost an apologetic way that she was surprised sometimes to feel "I hate to say it, but alone."

> Before you had a kind of touchstone where you could say, "Is it the right thing or not the right thing? Is there something that would be better?" But now you know you cannot always be reaching down to get affirmation. Everyone is reaching up to you. . . . You are the final decision-maker now. Up to that point you can always blame it on the chief. But once you're the chief . . . there are very few people you can blame your decisions on. And the perception that I see is that not

> many people end up liking you as chief. Up until you get to that position they can still perceive that there is somebody beyond you that they could go to—to get the decision changed. But once you're there and you make the decision, that's it.[33]

One female Chief compared the difference between filling the number two position of Deputy Chief and the number one position of Chief. She implied that she had not fully understood how great the challenge would be when she was in the number one spot.

> I think when you are the number two, you always think you can do better than number one. Probably you don't have any clue about some of the more subtle political issues that you have to deal with as chief. I felt very capable to do the job as chief in areas like running the organization. Slam-dunk! The operational stuff is the easy part. The internal relationships, the union labor relationships, the community relationships—it's really the level where you have to critically understand your own values and philosophies, and you have to be willing to make the tough value-based decisions. When I was Deputy Chief, I can remember saying about the chief, "Ahhh, why can't he make a decision?" Now I understand what he was going through since I'm faced with the same problems and also find it hard sometimes to reach a decision.[34]

Another Chief agreed with the preceding comments, also emphasizing the ultimate responsibility for decisions made by any leader and the stress related to this: "To me, personnel issues are the most difficult to handle, are time consuming and often are emotionally draining. Many times they will have an affect on a person's life for a long, long time. You've got to make them though, no matter how hard." She also mentioned, as did several other women interviewed, the constant pressure related to "subtle" political issues.

> As a chief the worst of times was probably the political turmoil I found in my third year as chief . . . and all the political turmoil that led up to that . . . being caught up in that and trying to provide service and be loyal to your boss and calm the waters at the same time . . . seemed like every little thing and everybody was "on my

back." It was probably the worst part of my career overall—most stressful, most difficult, with a lot of issues that were very ugly.[35]

Ruth Ann C., who had vied for the top job, indicated that if anything would stop her from again trying for that position it would be the politics involved. "Probably my worst time was when I went through all that political stuff. . . . I would probably look for a city that had a city manager as opposed to a mayor or city council, because our city council and mayor got into quite a few beefs over filling the chief position."

Regardless of "beefs" from public officials or citizens, women are making it to the top. San Francisco Acting Deputy Chief Heather Fong, a twenty-five-year-member of the force, was selected to head that city's force. According to the National Center for Women & Policing, Fong is the first Asian woman and only the eighth woman to head the department of a large city. San Francisco Mayor Gavin Newsom indicated that Fong had been tapped for the job as a reward for her performance over the years. He also stated that Fong was "willing to make change, and this is a department that needs to be moving in a new direction."[36]

Another California city hired department veteran Lynne Johnson to replace its male Chief, who announced plans to retire. Johnson was the eighth female originally hired by the department and climbed the ranks to become the city's first woman Captain and Assistant Chief. "To reach the chief's job has been a dream of mine for a long time,"[37] Johnson said, further indicating that she had never really thought of herself as a pioneer even though she may be considered that by many other women in policing.

Still, while both female Chiefs of Police and Deputy Chiefs indicated that their jobs were more intense and demanding than they had expected and that there were times when they wondered how they survived, they did not regret having achieved their positions. "There aren't many of us. We've achieved something," one woman said proudly as she concluded her interview with the authors. Another agreed, stating, "We're role models for a younger generation of females who will enter the [law enforcement] profession. Whether we'd do this again, knowing the difficulties involved, is not the question. We attempted the almost impossible and made it possible."

Pioneers or role models—these women will be among the leaders of the future in law enforcement. As Julia Grimes pointed out, "One of my major responsibilities as director of the Alaska State Troopers is to develop the leadership for the future of this division. . . . What I am very proud of are the promotions I've made since I became the director. . . . I'm confident in their abilities to be leaders—not just supervisors, not just managers—but leaders."[38]

Perhaps that last statement sums up the issue of anyone being selected for the top positions in law enforcement agencies. The women may have known that their chances of reaching their goals were nearly impossible. A few have achieved their goals, however, and have made similar goals possible for future police women.

CHAPTER

6

▼

Advantages Women Bring to Law Enforcement

> There are times when we can do the job a whole lot better, and there are times when a male can do the job better. Many times in a really difficult arrest situation with an uncooperative male perpetrator, a women officer talking to the guy seems to calm him down a little.
>
> —Interview with a female Patrol Officer, March 2004

The law enforcement image has always been macho—a profession for big, tough men who fight crime and violence with strength and toughness. Over the last twenty-five years, however, law enforcement agencies have come to realize that the traditional reactive approach to crime was not effective. Developing a new police strategy, one where police have the support of the community, was imperative. The new strategy, called "community policing" (which grew out of the concepts of team policing, ministations, and problem-oriented policing), is a philosophy of policing that is based on the concept that police officers and private citizens working together in creative ways can solve community problems that relate to crime, fear of crime, social and physical disorder, and neighborhood decay. This concept requires police departments to be more flexible and democratic. Police work would not be incident-driven but would emphasize community problem solving, with its goal to solve the problem in order to eliminate incidents or annoyances to the community. It encourages techniques such as problem identification, problem analysis, and problem resolution.[1]

As early as 1995, Atlanta's Police Chief Beverly J. Harvard supported the concept of community policing and explained that she was a "prevention person." Her philosophy on preventing crime was to join forces with the community:

> You've got to get the community involved in the whole process. We've [police have] got to get involved . . . in terms of solving their problems, helping them deal with things that are not necessarily law enforcement issues at the time. Because if you don't help them address these things at the time, they will ultimately become my issues—law enforcement issues.[2]

Fairfax County, Virginia, Acting Police Chief Lieutenant Colonel Suzanne G. Devlin indicated that she was most proud of her community policing strategies. According to a 2004 article in the *Fairfax Chronicle*, she helped set up a storefront office in the Franconia neighborhood, where police officers learned Spanish and worked with social workers. She also encouraged police to work in middle schools and high schools and believes it is important for the department's officers to "step up their contact with people."[3]

Although some law enforcement agencies continue to promote the paramilitary policing style of tough, aggressive behavior, this continues to result in poor community relations, abuse complaints, and, sometimes, violent confrontations. Diversifying a law enforcement agency by hiring women, who bring a different perspective to police work, has helped reduce problems connected with excessive use of force in arrests.

Defusing a bad situation by using good communication skills—by "talking it out"—can help officers in every aspect of their jobs. One of the strongest points for women police seems to be their ability to work well in the community. They appear to utilize what is called "community-oriented policing." This type of policing "represents a new approach to modern law enforcement, emphasizing communication and cooperation with citizens as well as informal problem solving."[4]

Harrington and Lonsway cite studies from 1987 and 2002 that show that, although female officers often have to use the same level of force as do male officers in carrying out their duties, women are "significantly less likely to be involved in employing both *deadly* force and *excessive* force."[5] Other research examined a report of the Independent Commission on the LAPD, which indicated that of those officers involved in excessive force, "only 3.4 percent were female, whereas women comprised 12.6 percent of the department."[6]

COMMUNICATION VERSUS FORCE

Verbal skills and equipment that officers now have at their disposal can be utilized in place of physical strength by both men and women to control a difficult situation. As one female officer stated in an interview,

> You know, for the most part, law enforcement now is if you have the right verbal skills, if you have the right tools. I can't tell you the last time I saw a use of force report where somebody really had to lay their hands on people. They are going to use pepper spray . . . a stun gun. They'll talk someone into calming down. So for me, strength is just a big cop out. . . . The biggest majority of what cops have to deal with has nothing to do with physical strength.[7]

Former Police Chief Penny Harrington and Katherine Spillar of the Feminist Majority Foundation (FMF; of which the NCWP is a division) also indicated that police women are less authoritarian and use excessive force less often than policemen. They emphasized the difference in policing philosophy of males versus females by citing researcher Joseph Balkin: "Policemen see police work as involving control through authority, while policewomen see it as a public service."[8]

Studies such as the one done in 2000 of the LAPD also support the contention that women cops are less prone to violence and indicate that women are better equipped to avoid violent confrontations than their male counterparts. For Harrington, the study merely confirmed her belief that women officers know how to defuse violence by calmly talking with those involved in police-related incidents:

> Women get the same kinds of calls that men get; it's just that from the time we're young we learn how to de-escalate violence. We're taught as young girls that when we're around people who are getting angry, what we need to do is calm them down. Women don't have their ego invested in winning a confrontation with someone. It's OK for us to back down or not come out as the strong person.[9]

State Trooper Laurie Hadley would agree with Harrington. "If it feels like I'm in what could turn out to be a troublesome situation, I'll try and talk myself and any other individual out of it. If you treat people cordially, with respect, usually you'll get that in return."

Another police woman indicated that "it's our natural tendency to listen and be a little more patient sometimes. We've come under a lot of criticism for doing it, but now that we look at community policing, that is exactly what they [departments] are telling you to do. To go out and problem solve."[10]

This is not to say that women police are "wimps." When the situation arises, they can also be tough. Five-foot, two-inch Adrienne Miller, who has been with the Alexandria, Virginia, Police Department for seven years, explained how women can be adaptable to the situation they face. "I think citizens perceive females as being more understanding, compassionate, even motherly," she stated in an interview for the *Christian Science Monitor*. "And they respond to this. . . . I know we are supposed to be more sensitive and communicate better, but I've seen female officers be mean and nasty just like male officers. . . . It's just a tough, tough profession."[11]

EXCESSIVE FORCE LAWSUITS

Apparently, the fact that many females utilize communication skills rather than physical force is of benefit to their departments, especially regarding complaints or possible lawsuits from citizens. According to Lonsway, because of their ability to communicate with the public, "women are substantially less likely to be named in a citizen complaint, sustained allegation or civil lawsuit for excessive use of force."[12]

Penny Harrington cited statistics in 2002 that "the average male officer is over eight and a half times more likely than his female counterpart to have an allegation of excessive force sustained against him, . . . is two to three times more likely than the average female officer to have a citizen name him in a complaint of excessive force, . . . [and] costs somewhere between two and a half times more than the average female officer in excessive force liability lawsuit payouts."[13]

In addition, a 2002 report from the FMF indicates a huge gender gap in police brutality. FMF Executive Vice President Spillar states, "Whether measured by citizen complaints, sustained allegations, or civil liability payouts in police brutality lawsuits, the average woman on patrol is less likely to use excessive force than the average man."[14] The 2002 research by Lonsway, Wood, and Spiller also states that, when there are excessive force lawsuits, female officers are cited at rates considerably below those of male officers, and "no female officers were named as defendants in cases of police officer involved sexual assault, sexual abuse, molestation, and domestic violence."[15]

Perhaps police department oral examinations should go a step further than they presently seem to do and ask both male and female recruits to demonstrate their skill in de-escalating a problem without the use of physical strength. This could often save departments the economic costs involved in having to defend against lawsuits filed by citizens for use of excessive force by police personnel.

A *Los Angeles Times* article provided statistics that showed that between 1990 and 1999 Los Angeles was required to pay out $63.4 million in lawsuits that accused male officers of excessive force, sexual assault, and domestic violence. By contrast, no female officers were named in sexual assault or domestic violence cases and "only $2.8 million was paid out on female officers for excessive-force lawsuits. . . . The dollar value of payouts in cases of excessive force and misconduct involving male LAPD officers exceeded that of payouts involving female officers by a ratio of 23 to 1."[16] Possibly hiring a substantial number of female police would help with the number of lawsuits filed and save the city a great deal of money, not to mention bad publicity for the city's law enforcement.

Los Angeles is not the only department to settle more excessive force lawsuits for men than for women officers. For the years 1996–2001, the San Jose, California, Police Department received 645 excessive force complaints for male officers, compared with 19 for female officers. In San Francisco, the figures for 1986–2001 were 5,488 for males and 401 for females. Across the country, in the Cincinnati, Ohio, Police Department, "male officers cost two and a half times more than female officers in terms of excessive force payouts, accounting for 92.3% of the dollars spent."[17]

WOMEN HELPING WOMEN

Domestic violence calls are among the most frequent received by police departments, are often the most difficult to deal with, and have long been considered the most dangerous for law enforcement personnel. Edwin J. Delattre emphasized in his book *Character and Cops* that, when responding to such calls, all officers should be "just in their treatment of the combatants, temperate in their use of force, compassionate to their victims."[18] However, he also stressed that being compassionate did not negate the use of sound judgment as officers usually had to deal with conflicting viewpoints regarding what had occurred.

There is a public perception that since women officers are often better at defusing potentially violent situations, they respond more effectively to domestic violence incidents than do male officers. Research tends to support this belief. A 1985 study in the *Journal of Criminal Justice* indicated that female police demonstrated more concern, patience, and understanding than their male counterparts, and the women who suffered the abuse rated the female officers more favorably.[19] In an article from the National Center for Women & Policing in 2003, it was reported that "all-male teams responding to victims who had previously called police received less favorable evaluations. . . . No such differences were seen when the responding officers included at least one woman."[20] The article goes on to cite Eleanor Smeal, the president of the FMF, who indicated that women bring more support for community policing than their male counterparts and respond more effectively to domestic violence cases.

According to the NCWP, statistics show that 2 to 3 million American women are physically assaulted each year by a male intimate, resulting in the single largest category of calls made to police. Response by police to these crimes of violence against females is critical, and the NCWP report stated that its research showed that female officers demonstrated more patience, concern, and understanding. In addition, battered women rated their contact with a female officer and the performance of the female as more helpful, more concerned, and more patient than the male officers' performance in these situations.[21]

Harrison, New York, Detective Liz VanHecke felt female officers tended to be more understanding in domestic disputes. However, she did state that she could calm males down better than she could females. "But," VanHecke said, "people will not cooperate with a female officer just based on gender. I think people just respect the uniform."[22]

One female Sergeant stated that she had been told by battered women that they were very glad a woman cop had come to their aid. "This was especially true," she said, "when they had reported several incidents of being abused. Apparently, they had seen policemen in the former incidents and felt the men hadn't really believed their stories."

Of course, not all female officers may be totally sympathetic. Parsons and Jeslow indicated that female officers occasionally didn't show much sympathy for female victims. They provided at least one opposing view of this from a woman with fifteen years' experience who had worked in both juvenile and child abuse units. According to her, female police officers tended to be somewhat critical of women who were victims of domestic abuse. She felt that, contrary to popular belief, most female police officers were women with strong personalities and wouldn't tolerate a man emotionally or physically abusing them. Therefore, she felt when the female officers encountered an abused female, they would ask, "Why the heck are you tolerating that?"[23]

It should also be pointed out that mandatory (or presumptive) arrest policies, which are now in effect in most states, do not necessarily provide a panacea to the problem of woman battering. In many cases, both parties involved in the dispute are arrested. As an example, both Connecticut and Rhode Island experienced an increase in dual arrests following the change to mandatory arrest. Also, in many instances both male and female officers may find it difficult to determine which spouse or partner was at fault in the dispute.[24] In this instance, whether the officers are sympathetic or not, both combatants may be arrested.

Another area where women police have been welcomed is dealing with rape cases. In the 1960s reported rapes almost doubled in number. One of the ways police departments responded to the public's concern about the increase was to assign more women officers to sex crime units. It is believed that there is some sort of natural empathy between female police officers and rape victims that can provide better communication. Because of this, the victims may be more willing to cooperate, which could result in more efficient evidence gathering. According to Horne, some police officials and citizens would like to see all-female-officer sex crime units or, at least, would like for only women to interview rape victims.[25] Today, many departments would like to require that a female officer be present to talk with rape victims. Unfortunately, many departments still have too few police women to meet such a requirement.

Lieutenant Michelle Sherwood, one of only two women in the Port Chester, New York, Police Department of sixty-five officers, discussed the advantages she and her colleague Melissa Acocella bring to interviews with female victims.

> I think we can talk to people without sounding as intimidating [as male officers]. . . . I think that [the women] are more comfortable with us, especially with a woman who has been raped. To have to divulge personal intimate aspects of what she has been through to a man when she has just been violated by a man . . . it's degrading on some emotional level, which is why we tend to deal with it.[26]

This is not to say that males cannot handle rape incidents with tact and sincerity. In fact, since there are still limited numbers of female officers in many departments, it will often be a male officer who makes the initial contact with a rape victim.

Yet another area where utilizing police women may be of great benefit is in cases of child abuse and child sexual abuse. As one male sergeant from a juvenile division explained,

> You have this little kid, many times three to four years old, and you send in a big male cop with a gun on his hip. . . . The child is scared to say anything. The policeman is intimidating. So, in our department we try, if one is available, to always make certain a policewoman or at least a woman from Social Services is involved. This often helps us get the needed information from the child. I don't know what the reason is . . . maybe the child relates better to a female . . . more like his or her mother.

From these examples, it would appear that police women simply do a better job in domestic violence, rape, and child abuse incidents. However, this appears to stereotype females, as was the case in earlier times. It seems to say that females should be used primarily in cases that deal with other females or children. While police women should be called for incidents such as these, they are very capable of handling *all types* of police work.

LEADERSHIP STYLES

A further advantage women bring to law enforcement is their leadership style—especially as they move into supervisory positions and achieve top ranks. In more than 160 studies of sex-related differences in leadership styles of men and women in various organizations, according to Eagly and Johnson only one difference was discovered. Women used a more participative or democratic style and a less autocratic or directive style than did men.[27]

One of the more widely recognized approaches utilized by women interviewed was the situational approach developed in the 1960s by P. Hersey and K. H. Blanchard. According to Peter G. Northouse, this style focuses on leadership in situations, utilizing the premise that different situations demand different styles of leadership.[28] As one woman explained,

> I learned . . . on the street that you cannot treat any two circumstances the same; you cannot treat any two citizens the same, and as I rose through the ranks, that you cannot treat any two subordinates or any two problems the same. You have got to have the flexibility to analyze the problem, research it . . . [find] a goal-setting strategy that works with the problem or the employee or the situation.[29]

According to Northouse, to determine what is needed in a particular situation, especially when dealing with personnel, a leader must recognize that skills and motivation vary over time. Situational leadership suggests that leaders should change the degree to which they are directive or supportive to meet the situation.[30]

Police Chief Ella Bully-Cummings believes that women find an alternate way to address various situations. She stated that she "has a more open leadership style" than her predecessor, who was often accused of heavy-handedness. "I don't want to say that women are more compassionate or humble or sensitive, . . . but there is a difference in the way we view a situation and we view tackling it."[31]

Participatory leadership, which refers to supervisors who allow subordinates to express their opinions and ideas and share in the decision-making process, is the style utilized by several women who have moved up in rank. Asked to describe the ideal Police Chief, Atlanta Police Chief Beverly J. Harvard said that a competent chief should be a good communicator who would stress participatory management and who would be flexible and open to change. "If you're the type of person who says, 'This is the way I do it, and I'm not flexible, and I'm not open to finding new ways,'" she insisted, "then you get bogged down and your department becomes stagnant."[32]

Like Harvard, Lieutenant Barbara Steinberg stressed, as the only female leader, that she was tough when she needed to be. "But also, I allow the men to help in the decision-making. I do not say, 'I am the Boss and that is that!' The men know I am the boss, and I have their respect. It is a team effort or squad effort, and we work together."[33]

This does not mean, however, that the female officer in a leadership position should not be able to make decisions on her own when occasions arise and to take responsibility for those decisions.

The head of Boston's Police Department, Commissioner Kathleen O'Toole, is said to be a combination of what it takes to be a good leader. She is considered to be tough, competitive, brainy, and politically astute. On the other hand, she is well suited to lead the department's community-policing initiative. As one spokesperson stated, "She has the common touch . . . the ability to empathize with people on a human level, and that's a great gift for a police commissioner."[34]

Chief Lynne Johnson felt that women in charge in police departments needed to be strong problem solvers and action oriented. In addition she felt these women had to be decision makers, not simply for the routine day-to-day decisions but "willing to make the tough decisions that will always arise in police work."[35]

"There are times when you have to be the voice of reason or the voice of calm," stated San Francisco Police Chief Heather Fong, the first Asian American female to head a big-city force. However, according to a member of that city's Chinese Chamber of Commere, she does not shrink from making necessary decisions. "A few years ago they had that movie 'Steel Magnolias'—that's a very appropriate term for her. People who have worked with her say she's very diligent and soft-spoken, but her resolve is as strong as steel."[36]

Women have proven themselves to be able to handle all types of police duty. They can work the streets, stop the barroom brawl, and be members of SWAT teams. But they also excel at handling domestic violence, rape, and child abuse incidents. They can be sympathetic yet tough in command positions. They truly are in the forefront of the relatively new concept called community policing.

CHAPTER 7

To Be a Successful Police Woman

> I just couldn't hack it—just couldn't take the pressure. I'm not talking about the job; I'm talking about all of the humiliating bantering, the gross comments, outright cruelty which came on a daily basis from the guys I worked with. They wanted me gone. I left!
>
> —Interview with a former female Deputy Sheriff, 2002

Obviously, while many women work in excellent police organizations and have rewarding careers as law enforcement officers, some simply are not successful. As several women indicated, the daily hassles and the lack of chances for upward mobility were not worth the few rewards that the job offered them.

The FMF cited a 2002 survey conducted by the NCWP that showed that "for the second consecutive year, the number of women in policing has declined. . . . The percentage of women in police agencies with 100 or more sworn officers remains small in 2001 at 12.7% . . . a decrease from 14.3% in 1999."[1]

Both male and female officers resign for many reasons. Louis M. Harris and J. Norman Baldwin list a number of primary sources of dissatisfaction cited by 58 officers who resigned from the Memphis, Tennessee, Police Department from 1975 through 1980 and 117 officers who voluntarily resigned from Vermont's Criminal Justice System in 1989. These included perceived lack of promotional opportunities, lack of appreciation for officers' efforts on the job, dissatisfaction with salary, fringe benefits, and retirement benefits, and dissatisfaction with personnel policies, administrative policies, and leadership styles of the chiefs.[2] As can be seen, these issues are all related to the internal environment rather than issues encountered when out on patrol. It is also interesting to note that a chart included in the study lists, as a reason for leaving, "reverse discrimination" and "morale problems" but does not list such reasons as "sexual harassment" or "hostile environment," which is still a problem in many agencies. As one female officer said, "The discrimination now—it's subtle and it's insidious. You are not always sure it's there, but it's definitely there. Still, it's kept real quiet. Now it's kind of behind-the-scenes quiet. It's so quiet you can't fight it. So in a way it's gotten worse."

An earlier study by L. J. Fry in the *Journal of Police Science and Administration* specifically addressed a nine-year period from one California Sheriff's Department and showed that 38 percent of female officers compared to 23 percent of male officers left to accept other law enforcement positions. Fry concluded that lack of opportunities for advancement might have been the chief reason for the higher turnover rate of police women.[3]

A study by the International Association of Chiefs of Police on retaining women officers noted that the women in that survey served, on average, five years before resigning, although quite a few left the profession after only two years. The top reason given for resignations was pregnancy (childbirth), family, or children. Other reasons cited included better opportunity, better pay, advancement, and career change.[4] A few women opted for other areas connected to law enforcement for which they felt more suited—probation, counseling, intervention, and so forth.

Some officers (male or female) resign because the work has gotten more violent. In discussions with police women during the interview process and at the Rocky Mountain Conference of Women in Law Enforcement, several, who had been in their careers for nine or ten years, indicated that the streets had become more dangerous, particularly in the larger metropolitan areas. Many had noticed the more aggressive attitude of young people they encountered in various situations. Some mentioned the problems with gang activity. They perceived a considerable increase in gun usage among juveniles, specifically drive-by shootings or shoot-outs with the police. They also emphasized the lack of respect they received even when they showed respect for people involved in deviant behavior. However, it was not just that individuals encountered in arrest situations tended to be rude or use vulgar and abusive language; it was the threat of physical violence that worried them most.

"I've been called everything you can think of," one woman explained, with nods of assent from those seated near her. "That isn't pleasant, but you just shrug it off. It's just part of the job, something you almost expect. But, when I get punched or kicked, especially time after time, that gets your attention. It doesn't mean that I'm leaving the job, but I do think about leaving my kids without a mother, if such a situation or a worse one should occur."

LIFE WITH THE BADGE

The larger proportion of women who opt to be cops stay and say that they love their job. These women who have "been there, done that" know what it takes to wear the blue uniform. During interviews and through answers to questionnaires they shared numerous tips on what women could do to prepare to enter law enforcement. A few of these comments are listed below.

Research the Job

Get an idea of what it really means to be a police officer. Do an internship or join the police reserves. Get an idea of what it mean to be a police officer before applying for a job. As some officers explained,

> If you have an opportunity to go through a citizens' academy, . . . ride along [with police officers] and get some education about it. Know what you are going to be doing. . . . Being a [police] cadet gave me that advantage of learning something about the culture and the unspoken rules before I actually went into it.[5]

Be Committed

Go after your dream and your passion. "And if you are going to take the job, make a true commitment," one officer stated, "because if . . . you really feel like as soon as it gets tough or as soon as I am tired of working the shifts or tired of working holidays, then I am going to bail. Then you are really selling yourself short, and it is a commitment that really ends up hurting the department. So I think you have to really be committed, be willing to take some risks."[6]

Understand the Service You Will Have to Provide

The people police officers serve may not be the people they like best. They daily deal with the problems of society. One female officer explained the situations in which she finds herself.

> We see homicides; we see rape victims; we see sudden infant death syndrome victims. So you have to change because we normally don't grow up in those worlds. And then you get here and you have to toughen up. You can't go on a call and cry like a baby . . . where you have seen something so devastating that there is some emotion to it . . . you have to harden yourself somewhat so that you don't . . . go crazy with all the stuff—that you have to still balance that with some compassion.[7]

Be Prepared to Make Tough Decisions

An officer may have to take a child away from his or her parents or to kill someone in the line of duty.

Don't Lose Your Femininity to Fit the Male Mold

As a Master Officer from Colorado stated, "You are not one of the boys. You cannot *be* one of the boys. Be yourself and be the best officer you can be. Then you will succeed." Detective Mianna Sorensen felt that women could be officers and not give up family life. "Don't be afraid to have a baby and a family," she stated. "Your life is first."[8]

Many additional points were emphasized by almost all the women interviewed (or who completed questionnaires) and include the following:

- Be prepared to face hostility, sometimes in the workplace and often in public situations. Develop a thick skin.
- Develop human relations skills.
- Get a mentor, if possible, and be a mentor.
- Network, which is especially important for top positions such as Chief of Police.
- Continue with your education, both inside and outside the department.
- Take different positions within the department, which may enhance chances for promotion.
- Study and be prepared for promotional exams and take all positions offered.
- Develop a reputation for a strong work ethic and demonstrate integrity.
- Understand that you will be working shifts and holidays and that promotion may bring shift work.
- Support zero tolerance for any type of harassment or discrimination.
- If trying to reach the top of the ladder, be sure to network and develop external support systems.

In her article "Advice to Women Beginning a Career in Law Enforcement," retired Chief Penny Harrington also gave some advice to those entering the career field, including:

- Always tell the truth. A police officer's credibility is of the utmost importance.
- Don't complain about your job to your coworkers.
- Stay current on police matters.
- Keep in good physical condition.
- Be good to yourself. Practice stress-reduction techniques.
- Join a women police organization such as the National Center for Women & Policing or the International Association of Women Police.[9]

Two women who have had successful careers in law enforcement probably gave some of the most valuable advice and encouragement to females entering that profession. "You have an opportunity to make a difference, and I think that, overall, that is what sustains me in this work," one individual said. "You really can make a difference and that is the overall motivation for moving up the ranks in my mind. At each level you can make a larger contribution not only to the organization but to the community and really see the impact of your work."[10]

"Probably the first lesson is don't ever quit," stressed the second police woman. "Don't ever say you can't. If somebody else says you just can't do that, whatever the reason is, and this is something you want to do, then go after your dream. Go after your passion; make it come true. . . . It might take some extra work; it's not going to always be easy, but only you can do that."[11]

Being a police officer is not an easy job, for males or females. No one would say that it is. As Edwin J. Delattre wrote, "Living up to the public trust is demanding work. It can involve disappointment, weariness, and stress."[12] It can take a toll on individuals' physical and emotional health and that of their families. It is a job that demands dedication.

However, those who enter the profession provide a valuable service to their communities. Individuals wearing the badge are usually the first persons called in time of trouble. While they see the seamier side of life—the shootings, the rapes, the drugs—that is a part of deviant behavior, they also are able to see the comfort and feeling of security they give to the public. Although they began strictly as caregivers for deviant females and juveniles, women have been able to hold their own in the ranks and are now making inroads into the top police positions. Tell some of the histories, advises Sergeant Lisa Grosskrueger, and this is an important point. "We *must not* forget. If we do not document, future generations will not believe what women have accomplished."[13]

And women have accomplished a great deal. For women entering what is still considered by some to be a macho, paramilitary career suitable only for men, there are many other citizens, as well as colleagues, who have come to accept and are extremely supportive of women's growing role in policing. Ideally women will heed the advice given by those who already have been successful in their jobs, and, as in the past, will continue to decide on careers in law enforcement. They, like their male peers, will become role models for other women as they provide needed service and support to their fellow officers and to their communities. Perhaps officer Jean Marie Bready summed it up best when she said, "There is nothing more fabulous than a strong woman in a police uniform."

APPENDIX 1

Questionnaire (March–May 2004)

This questionnaire was sent via e-mail to police women throughout the United States who were listed as members of the National Center for Women & Policing.

1. When and why did you enter into a law enforcement career?
2. Were you recruited?
3. How does your department recruit women?
4. What is your education level?
5. What is your rank?
6. What is the size of your agency and the population of your community?
7. How many women are in your department?
8. How many women are in command positions?
9. Do you wish to advance to Chief of Police? Why or why not?
10. Have you had any bad (or good) gender issues?
11. Have you had any lawsuits in your agency? Explain.
12. What are the leadership styles of women in charge (if any) in your agency?
13. What advantages do women bring to law enforcement?
14. Did you have a mentor or mentors?
15. Do you network?
16. What are the qualities that women need to be good police officers?

17. Briefly describe the worst time you have had as an officer.
18. Briefly describe the best time you have had as an officer.
19. Why aren't more women joining law enforcement agencies?
20. What advice do you offer females entering this career?

APPENDIX 2

Questionnaire (September 2004)

Those attending the Rocky Mountain Conference for Women in Law Enforcement were asked whether they would be willing to complete this questionnaire. It was kept brief due to the fact that the attendees had heavy schedules and would probably complete the questionnaire after night seminars or dinners.

1. Comment on promotions for women.
   Have you promoted?
   Do you wish to promote and how high?
   Have you had difficulties with the promotion process? Please explain.
2. What do you perceive is the most difficult problem facing women entering this profession today?
3. What do you feel has been your most difficult experience(s) on the job?
4. Please list a few specific issues you feel should be included in a book about women in law enforcement.

Notes

CHAPTER 1: FROM PRISON MATRON TO POLICE CHIEF

1. Dorothy Moses Schulz, "Invisible No More: A Social History of Women in U.S. Policing," in *The Criminal Justice System and Women: Offenders, Prisoners, Victims, and Workers*, 3rd ed., edited by Barbara Raffel Price and Natalie J. Sokoloff (Boston: McGraw-Hill, 2004), 484.

2. Ibid.

3. Ibid.; Dorothy Moses Schulz, "California Dreaming: Leading the Way to Gender-Free Police Management," *CJ The Americas* 7, no. 1 (1994): 8–10.

4. B. L. Berg and K. J. Budnick, "Defeminization of Women in Law Enforcement: A New Twist in the Traditional Police Personality," *Journal of Police Science and Administration* 14 (1986): 314.

5. Ibid.; Marion E. Gold, *Top Cops: Profiles of Women in Command* (Chicago: Brittany Publications, 1999), 17.

6. Gloria E. Myers, *A Municipal Mother: Portland's Lola Greene Baldwin, America's First Policewoman* (Corvallis: Oregon State University Press, 1995), 8–14; Barbara Raffel Price and Susan Gavin, "A Century of Women in Policing," in *The Criminal Justice System and Women*, edited by B. R. Price and N. Sokoloff (New York: Clark Boardman, 1982), 399.

7. In taking the oath, it must be assumed that Baldwin was sworn in as a police officer. Police departments also utilize personnel who are not sworn officers; these can include clerks, secretaries, dispatchers, evidence custodians, and the like.

8. Myers, *Municipal Mother*, 21–22.

9. Dorothy Moses Schulz, *From Social Worker to Crimefighter: Women in United States Municipal Policing* (Westport, CT: Praeger, 1995), 23–24.

10. Ibid., 25.

11. Ibid.; Dorothy Moses Schulz, "The Police Matron Movement: Paving the Way for Policewomen," *Police Studies: The International Review of Police Development* 12, no. 3 (1989): 115–124; C. Fletcher, *Breaking and Entering: Women Cops Talk About Life in the Ultimate Men's Club* (New York: HarperCollins, 1995), xv; Sean A. Grennan, "The Past, Present, and Future of Women in Policing," in *It's a Crime: Women and Justice*, 2nd ed., edited by Roslyn Muraskin (Upper Saddle River, NJ: Prentice Hall, 2000), 384.

12. Schulz, *From Social Worker to Crimefighter*, 26–27, 43; Price and Gavin, "A Century of Women in Policing."

13. Peter Horne, *Women in Law Enforcement*, 2nd ed. (Springfield, IL: Charles C. Thomas, 1980), 90–91.

14. Schulz, *From Social Worker to Crimefighter*, 27.

15. Elizabeth Munger, "Policewomen for Smaller Cities," *Woman Citizen* 10, no. 4 (July 11, 1925): 15.

16. GeoCities, "First Woman Sheriffs in the United States of America," http://www.geocities.com/vbenson_2000/sheriffs.htm (accessed April 2, 2004); material also from two books by Leona Bruce on Bannister *Bannister Was There* [1968] and *Four Years in the Coleman Jail, Daughter of Two Sheriffs* [1982] listed on the Handbook of Texas Online, http://www.tsha.utexas.edu/handbook/online/articles/view/BB/fbacq.html; Bob Hansen, "Lady Sheriff an Unofficial Official," *The Hawk Eye*, July 23, 2000, http://www.thehawkeye.com/columns.Hansen/2000/cha72300.html; Ionia County, "History of the Ionia County [Michigan] Office of Sheriff," http://www.ioniacounty.org/sheriff/Sheriff_history.asp (accessed April 2, 2004).

17. Susan Ehrlich Martin and Nancy C. Jurik, *Doing Justice, Doing Gender* (Thousand Oaks, CA: Sage Publications, 1996), 56–57.

18. Geocities, "Important Firsts in Women's Law Enforcement," http://www.geocities.com/vbenson_2000/firsts.htm (accessed May 3, 2004).

19. Schulz, *From Social Worker to Crimefighter*, 80.

20. Horne, *Women in Law Enforcement*, 30–31.

21. August Vollmer, "Meet the Lady Cop," *Survey*, March 15, 1930. This article also mentions the fact that a 1929 institute on police administration at Riverside, California, was well attended by both men and women; however, the number of women in attendance was not provided, nor does the article indicate whether any of the women were in administrative positions.

22. Mary E. Hamilton, "Woman's Place in the Police Department," *American City* 32 (February 1925): 194.

23. Schulz, *From Social Worker to Crimefighter*, 80.

24. Ibid., 98–99; Karl Detzer, "Detroit's Lady Cops," *American Mercury* (March 1942): 345–351.

25. Irma Wann Buwalda, "The Policewoman—Yesterday, Today and Tomorrow," *Journal of Social Hygiene* 31, no. 5 (May 1945): 290–293.

26. Schulz, "Invisible No More," 484.

27. Ibid.

28. Fletcher, *Breaking and Entering*.

29. Gold, *Top Cops*, 20.

30. Ibid.

31. Ibid., 21.

32. "Women to Ride in Police Cruisers," *Memphis Press-Scimitar*, January 12, 1970, http://www.memphispolice.org/Women%20inPolicing%20-%IN%the20News (accessed May 25, 2004).

33. Larry J. Siegel, *Criminology*, 2nd ed. (New York: West, 1985), 507.

34. Martin and Jurik, *Doing Justice, Doing Gender*, 58–59.

35. Susan E. Martin, "The Interactive Effects of Race and Sex on Women Police Officers," in Price and Sokoloff, *Criminal Justice System and Women*, 533.

36. Retired Deputy Chief Charlene Graham, interview with the authors, June 2004.

37. Schulz, *From Social Worker to Crime Fighter*; Gold, *Top Cops*, 22.

38. Gold, *Top Cops*.

39. Schulz, "Police Matron Movement," 117.

40. Horne, *Women in Law Enforcement*, 37–38.

41. U.S. Army Women's Museum, History of Army Women, Significant Dates (1976–1985), http://www.awm.lee.army.mil/Army (accessed October 2, 2002).

42. Fletcher, *Breaking and Entering*; Price and Gavin, "A Century of Women in Policing."

43. Gold, *Top Cops*, 24.

44. Alida V. Merko, Kate Bagley, and Michele C. Bafuma, "In Defense of Affirmative Action for Women in the Criminal Justice Professions," in Muraskin, *It's a Crime*, 80.

45. Schulz, "Invisible No More," 491.

46. Gold, *Top Cops*, 27.

47. Georgia Sheriffs' Association, http://www.georgiasheriffs.org/off sheriff.html (accessed April 2, 2004).

48. U.S. Department of Justice (Bureau of Justice Statistics), http://www.ojp.usdoj.gov/bjs/pub/ascii/sd97.txt (accessed April 2, 2004).

49. M. A. Fuoco, "City Force No. 1 in Women in Blue," *Pittsburgh Post-Gazette*, May 28, 1998, A1–A10.

50. Ibid.

51. "The Future of Women in Policing: Mandates for Action," International Association of Chiefs of Police bulletin, November 1998, 1.

52. Donna C. Hale and Mark Lanier, "The Next Generation: Women in Policing in the Twenty-First Century," in *Visions for Change: Crime and Justice in the Twenty-First Century*, 2nd ed. edited by Roslyn Muraskin and Albert R. Roberts (Upper Saddle River, NJ: Prentice Hall, 1999), 402.

53. "Hiring and Retaining More Women: The Advantages to Law Enforcement Agencies," National Center for Women & Policing bulletin, Spring 2003, 2. http://www.pennyharrington.com/hireandretain.htm (accessed May 25, 2004).

54. "Number of Women in Policing Decreasing: Enormous Gender Gap Found in Rate of Police Brutality," National Center for Women & Policing, March 8, 2004, http://www.womenandpolicing.org/article.asp?id=6499 (accessed May 5, 2004).

55. Ibid.

CHAPTER 2: BREACHING THE BLUE WALL

1. Thomas L. Austin and Don Hummer, "What Do College Students Think of Policewomen? An Attitudinal Assessment of Future Law Enforcement Personnel," *Women and Criminal Justice* 10, no. 4 (1999): 4.

2. Sandra K. Wells, "Women in Policing: The Experience of Female Police Chiefs and Deputy Police Chiefs" (PhD diss., Colorado State University, 2001), 59.

3. Donna Leinwand, "Lawsuits of '70s Shape Current Police Leadership," *USA Today*, http://usatoday.printthis.clickability.com/pt/cpt?action=cpt&title=USATODAY.com+-+L (accessed September 9, 2004).

4. M. Vega and I. Silverman, "Female Police Officers as Viewed by Their Male Counterparts," *Police Science* (May 1982): 31–39; Susan Erhlich Martin, *Breaking and Entering: Policewomen on Patrol* (Berkeley: University of California Press, 1980); D. J. Bell, "Policewomen: Myths and Reality," *Journal of Police Science and Administration* 10 (1982): 112–120.

5. Austin and Hummer, "What Do College Students Think?" 18.

6. Venessa Garcia, " 'Difference' in the Police Department," *Journal of Contemporary Criminal Justice* 19, no. 3 (August 2003): 336.

7. Los Angeles Police Department, "Civil Rights Consent Decree Overview," http://www.lapdonline.org/inside_lapd/cd/consent_decree.htm (accessed May 3, 2004).

8. "Equality Denied: The Status of Women in Policing: 2001," National Center for Women & Policing bulletin, April 2002, 11.

9. Garcia, "'Difference' in the Police Department," 336.

10. "LAPD Announces New Initiative to Increase Women Officers," *Women & Policing News Wire*, December 17, 2002, http://www.womenandpolicing.org/article.asp?id=7370 (accessed March 8, 2004).

11. "Evaluation of the Impact of Affirmative Action Policies on Women in Law Enforcement," http://www.geocities.com/CapitolHill/8512/eval.html (accessed May 3, 2004).

12. Leinwand, "Lawsuits of '70s."

13. Peter Horne, *Women in Law Enforcement*, 2nd ed. (Springfield, IL: Charles C. Thomas, 1980), 184.

14. Jennifer Brown and Frances Heidensohn, *Gender and Policing: Comparative Perspectives* (New York: St. Martin's Press, 2000), 131.

15. Molly Snyder Edler, "Milwaukee Talks: Nan Hegerty," March 9, 2004, On Milwaukee.com, http://www.onmilwaukee.com/articles/print/hegertytalks.html (accessed September 15, 2004).

16. Tataboline Brant, "Trooper Director Proud of Her Troops," *Anchorage Daily News*, February 1, 2004, http://www.adn.com/alaska/story/4694326p-4645722c.html (accessed September 8, 2004).

17. Ibid.

18. California Highway Patrol, "From Secretary to Safeguarding the Public," http://www.chp.ca.gov/recruiting/html.bonnie_stanton.html (accessed September 17, 2004).

19. Deputy Police Chief (retired) Charlene Graham, interview with the authors, June 2004.

20. Sergeant Darlene Rogers, questionnaire, August 17, 2004 (see Appendix 1).

21. Chief Lynne Johnson, questionnaire, August 17, 2004 (see Appendix 1).

22. "Recruiting Women," *Police Chief*, April 2002, http://www.iwitts.com/html/the_police_chief_magazine_rec.html.

23. Joan C. Barker, *Danger, Duty, and Disillusion: The Worldview of Los Angeles Police Officers* (Prospect Heights, IL: Waveland Press, 1999), 8–9.

24. Trooper Laurie Hadley, interview with the authors, February 5, 2002.

25. Wells, *Women in Policing*, 49.

26. Lieutenant Barbara Steinberg, questionnaire, May 18, 2004 (see Appendix 1).

27. Wells, *Women in Policing*, 49–50.

28. Ibid., 50.

29. Deputy Police Chief (retired) Charlene Graham, interview with the authors, June 2004.

30. Officer Jean Marie Bready, questionnaire, 2004 (see Appendix 1).

31. Michael Armstrong, "Homer Woman Graduates from Public Safety Academy," *Homer News*, June 10, 2004, http://homernews.com/stories/061004/new_061004new014001.shtml (accessed September 8, 2004).

32. Chanda Sommers, interview with the authors, July 2004.

33. Washington Association of Sheriffs and Police Chiefs, "Assessment Centers," http://www.waspc.org/assessment.shtml (accessed September 9, 2004).

34. Barker, *Danger, Duty, and Disillusion*, 10.

35. Martin, *Breaking and Entering*, 47.

36. Penny Harrington, *Triumph of the Spirit* (Chicago: Brittany Publications, 1999), 119.

37. Joseph Polisar and Donna Milgram, "Recruiting, Integrating and Retaining Women Police Officers: Strategies That Work," *Police Chief*, October 1998, http://www.iwitts.com/html/the_police_chief_magazine_str.html (accessed May 25, 2004); Donna Milgram, "Recruiting Women to Policing: Practical Strategies That Work," *Police Chief*, April 2002, http://www.iwitts.com/html/the_police_chief_magazine_rec.html (accessed May 25, 2004).

38. Marisa Silvestri, *Women in Charge: Policing, Gender and Leadership* (Portland, OR: Willan, 2003), 35.

39. "Pennsylvania Police Ignore Progressive Physical Testing Trends," *Women & Policing News Wire*, December 29, 2002, http://www.womenandpolicing.org/article.asp?id=7371 (accessed March 8, 2004).

40. Ibid.

41. Kimberly Lonsway, "Tearing Down the Wall: Problems with Consistency, Validity, and Adverse Impact of Physical Agility Testing in Police Selection," *Police Quarterly* 6, no. 3 (September 2003): 6.

42. Ibid., 3.

43. Ibid., 6.

44. Ibid., 7.

45. Lynn O'Shaughnessy, "Police Academy Training Has Changed to Accommodate Women," *Memphis Press-Scimitar*, 1980, http://www

.memphispolice.org?Women%20-%20In%20the%20News (accessed May 25, 2004).

46. Lynn O'Shaughnessy, "'Weaker Sex' Police Cadets Put Cloud on Training Program," *Memphis Press-Scimitar*, 1980, http://www.memphis police.org/Women%20in%20Policing%20-%20In%20the%20News (accessed May 25, 2004).

47. Horne, *Women in Law Enforcement*, 159.

48. Wells, *Women in Policing*, 59.

49. Police Officer II, Missouri, questionnaire, September 24, 2004 (see Appendix 2).

50. Ibid.

51. National Center for Women and Policing, 1999.

52. Leinwand, "Lawsuits of '70s."

53. Joseph Balkin, "Why Policemen Don't Like Policewomen," *Journal of Police Science and Administration* 16, no. 1 (1988): 29–38.

54. Gwendolyn L. Gerber, *Women and Men Police Officers: Status, Gender, and Personality* (Westport, CT: Praeger, 2001), 1.

55. Pat Heim, *Hardball for Women* (New York: Plume, 1992), 8.

56. Brown and Heidensohn, *Gender and Policing*, 74–75.

57. Wells, *Women in Policing*, 61.

58. Ibid.

59. Steinberg, questionnaire.

60. Rogers, questionnaire.

61. Questionnaire, 2004; Wells, *Women in Policing*, 85.

62. Barker, *Danger, Duty, and Disillusion*, 6, 13.

63. Bready, questionnaire.

64. Rogers, questionnaire.

65. Wells, *Women in Policing*, 58.

66. Ibid.

67. "The Future of Women in Policing: Mandates for Action," International Association of Chiefs of Police bulletin, November 1998, 16.

68. Brown and Heidensohn, *Gender and Policing*, 144.

69. Lieutenant Deborah J. Cady, questionnaire, September 23, 2004 (see Appendix 2).

70. Kristin Touchstone, questionnaire, 2004 (see Appendix 1); Bready, questionnaire.

71. W. Richard Stephens, *Careers in Criminal Justice*, 2nd ed. (Boston: Allyn and Bacon, 2002), 17.

CHAPTER 3: FACING CHALLENGES

1. "Equality Denied: The Status of Women and Policing" (Los Angeles: National Center for Women and Policing, 1999), 1–5.

2. J. Lieberman, "The Effects of Sex Bias in the Evaluation of Police Reports, 1989" (manuscript).

3. Bill D'Agostino, "City to Hire First Female Police Chief," *Palo Alto Weekly*, February 7, 2003, http://www.paloaltoonline.com/weekly/morgue/2003/2003_02_07.qchief07mb.html (accessed August 29, 2004).

4. Elizabeth Simpson Smith, *Breakthrough: Women in Law Enforcement* (New York: Walker, 1982), 8.

5. Susan Ehrlich Martin, *Breaking and Entering: Police Women on Patrol* (Berkeley: University of California Press, 1980), 92.

6. Ibid.

7. Joan C. Barker, *Danger, Duty, and Disillusion: The Worldview of Los Angeles Police Officers* (Prospect Heights, IL: Waveland, 1999), 197.

8. Ibid., 197–198.

9. Connie Fletcher, *Breaking and Entering: Women Cops Talk about Life in the Ultimate Men's Club* (New York: HarperCollins, 1995), 153.

10. Sandra K. Wells, "Women in Policing: The Experience of Female Police Chiefs and Deputy Police Chiefs" (PhD diss., Colorado State University, 2001), 70.

11. Martin, *Breaking and Entering*, 200.

12. Katherine Stuart Van Wormer and Clemens Bartollas, *Women and the Criminal Justice System* (Boston: Allyn and Bacon, 2000), 173.

13. Ibid.

14. Wells, "Women in Policing," 63.

15. Ibid., 63–64.

16. Penny Harrington, *Triumph of the Spirit* (Chicago: Brittany Publications, 1999), 25.

17. Van Wormer and Bartollas, *Women and the Criminal Justice System*, 174.

18. S. E. Burns, "Issues in Workplace Sexual Harassment Law and Related Social Science Research," *Author's Abstract Journal of Social Science*, no. 51 (1995): 194.

19. "More Women Police File Sex Discrimination Suits," *Women & Policing News Wire*, August 19, 1999, http://www.womenandpolicing.org/article.asp?id=398 (accessed March 8, 2004).

20. "MA Women Officers File Sex Discrimination Suit," *Women & Policing News Wire*, November 7, 2002, http://www.womenandpolicing.org/

article.asp?id=7259 (accessed March 8, 2004); "Three Female Police Officers Win $2.5 Million Sex Harassment Suit," *Women & Policing News Wire*, June 6, 2003, http://www.womenandpolicing.org/article.asp?id=7839 (accessed March 8, 2004).

21. Jenn Abelson, "Trooper Files Sex-Bias Claim," *Boston Globe*, January 20, 2004, B1.

22. "Sexual Harassment Allegations Believed to Have Caused Chief's Resignation," *Women & Policing News Wire*, August 16, 2002, http://www.womenandpolicing.org/article.asp?id=6797 (accessed March 8, 2004).

23. "Female Police Officer Reinstated after Three-Year Sexual Harassment Battle," *Women & Policing News Wire*, July 25, 2002, http://www.womenandpolicing.org/article.asp?id=6729 (accessed March 8, 2004).

24. Jennifer Lynn Gossett and Joyce E. Williams, "Perceived Discrimination among Women in Law Enforcement," *Women & Criminal Justice* 10 (1998): 58.

25. Fletcher, *Breaking and Entering*, 132–133.

26. Jennifer Weil, "Women Police Are on the Beat, but Not in Force," *Journal News*, The Item, May 7, 2004, http://www.thejournalnews.com/weekly050704/a0lit0507femalec.html (accessed September 9, 2004).

27. "Workplace Issues: Recognizing Workplace Discrimination," National Center for Women & Policing, http://www.womenandpolicing.org/workplace2~harassment.asp (accessed March 25, 2004).

28. "Workplace Issues: Pregnancy Issues in Law Enforcement," National Center for Women & Policing, May 25, 2004, http://www.womenandpolicing.org/workplace4~pregnancy.asp (accessed May 25, 2004); "Facts about Pregnancy Discrimination," U.S. Equal Employment Opportunity Commission, http://www.eeoc.gov/facts/fs-preg.html (accessed March 25, 2004).

29. Ibid.

30. Sergeant Darlene Rogers, questionnaire, September 2004 (see Appendix 1).

31. "$1 Million Awarded to MA State Troopers in Pregnancy Discrimination Case," *Women & Policing News Wire*, October 8, 2002 (citing an Associated Press article, October 5, 2002), http://www.womenandpolicing.org/article.asp?id=7058 (accessed March 8, 2004).

32. "Two WA Women Police Officers Sue Police Department for Discrimination," *Women & Policing News Wire*, August 16, 2002, http://www.womenandpolicing.org/article.asp?id=6796 (accessed March 8, 2004).

33. "Veteran Woman Police Officer Claims Gender Discrimination," *Women & Policing News Wire*, June 26, 2003 (citing both the *Boston Globe*

and the Associated Press), http://www.womenandpolicing.org/article.asp?id=7885 (accessed March 8, 2004).

34. Abelson, "Trooper Files Sex-Bias Claim."

35. Maria Cramer, "Female Officer Files Harassment Lawsuit," *Boston Globe*, March 28, 2004, 1.

36. "Jury Awards over $3 Million."

37. Ibid.

38. Gossett and Williams, "Perceived Discrimination," 63.

39. Ibid., 64.

40. Jennifer Brown and Frances Heidensohn, *Gender and Policing: Comparative Perspectives* (New York: St. Martin's Press, 2000), 103.

41. Susan E. Martin, "The Interactive Effects of Race and Sex on Women Police Officers," in *The Criminal Justice System and Women: Offenders, Prisoners, Victims, and Workers*, 3rd ed., edited by Barbara Raffel Price and Natalie J. Sokoloff (Boston: McGraw-Hill, 2004), 527.

42. Ibid., 528.

43. Ibid., 532–534.

44. Ibid., 534

45. Ibid.

46. Cited in Penny Harrington and Kimberly A. Lonsway, "Current Barriers and Future Promise for Women in Policing," in Price and Sokoloff, *Criminal Justice System and Women*, 498.

47. Susan Ehrlich Martin and Nancy C. Jurik, *Doing Justice, Doing Gender: Women in Law and Criminal Justice Occupations* (Thousand Oaks, CA: Sage Publications, 1996), 58.

48. "Workplace Issues: Recognizing Workplace Discrimination."

49. Susan L. Miller, Kay B. Forest, and Nancy C. Jurik, "Lesbians in Policing: Perceptions and Work Experiences with the Macho Cop Culture," in Price and Sokoloff, *Criminal Justice System and Women*, 516.

50. Robin A. Buhrke, *A Matter of Justice: Lesbians and Gay Men in Law Enforcement* (New York: Routledge, 1996), 19.

51. Erik Meers, "Good Cop Gay Cop: From the Beat Patrol to the Precinct House, Gay and Lesbian Police Officers Are Shattering the Blue Wall of Silence," *Advocate*, March 3, 1998, http://www.find articles.com/p/articles/mi_m1589/is_n754ai_20350566 (accessed August 17, 2004).

52. Buhrke, *Matter of Justice*, 18–19.

53. Miller, Forest, and Jurik, "Lesbians in Policing," 516–517.

54. Ibid., 37.

55. Buhrke, *Matter of Justice*, 98–99.

56. Meers, "Good Cop, Gay Cop."

57. Ibid.

58. UK Home Office, "Gay and Lesbian and Sexuality Issues," http://www.homeoffice.gov.uk/crimpol/police/equality/sexualityissues.html (accessed August 17, 2004).

59. GOAL—Gay Officers Action League, http://www.goalny.org/mission.htm (accessed August 17, 2004); Denver Public Safety Recruitment, "Denver Police Department Employee Groups," http://www.denvergov.org/Recruit/template113569.asp (accessed August 17, 2004); Gay Police Officers Action League of DC, http://www.goaldc.com/ (accessed August 17, 2004).

60. Harrington and Lonsway, "Current Barriers," 504.

61. Michael Hughes and Carolyn J. Kroehler, *Sociology: The Core*, 7th ed. (Boston: McGraw-Hill, 2005), 267–268.

62. Mary Ann Lamanna and Agnes Riedmann, *Marriages and Families: Making Choices and Facing Change*, 5th ed. (Belmont, CA: Wadsworth, 1994), 443–445.

63. Martin, *Breaking and Entering*, 200.

64. Terry Constant, "Not So Obvious Police Stress," http://www.tearsofacop.com/police/articles/constant.html (accessed August 17, 2004).

65. Kevin M. Gilmartin, "Emotional Survival for Law Enforcement," paper delivered at the Rocky Mountain Women in Law Enforcement Conference, Pueblo, Colorado, September 22–24, 2004.

66. Dan Goldfarb, "The Effects of Stress on Police Officers," http://www.heavybadge.com/efstress.htm (accessed August 17, 2004). Dr. Goldfarb works for Suffolk, New York's Police Benevolent Association Psychological Services and has written articles for *Off Duty Magazine* on stress and post traumatic stress.

67. Constant, "Not So Obvious Police Stress."

68. Kevin M. Gilmartin, *Emotional Survival for Law Enforcement: A Guide for Officers and Their Families* (Tucson, AZ: E-S Press, 2002), 113–131; and information presented at Rocky Mountain Women in Law Enforcement Conference, Pueblo, Colorado, September 22–24, 2004.

69. Chuck Pratt (Police Chief, retired), "Why Do Police Officers Have Such an Outlandish Rate of Marital and Domestic Failure and Calamity?" http://www.geocities.com/~halbrown/police_affairs.html (accessed August 14, 2004).

70. "Female Police Psychology," *Detroit News*, 1997, http://www.angelfire.com/vt/policepsychology/page5.html (accessed August 29, 2004).

71. Michael G. Aamodt and Nicole A. Stalnaker, "Police Officer Suicide: Frequency and Officer Profiles," http://www.radford.edu/~maamodt/PoliceResearch/PoliceSuicide.pdf (accessed August 29, 2004).

72. "NYC Police Less Likely to Commit Suicide Than NYC Citizens, New York Weill Cornell Study Shows," http://www.med.cornell.edu/news/press/2002/12_19_02_b.html (accessed August 29, 2004).

73. Aamodt and Stalnaker, "Police Officer Suicide."

74. "NYC Police Less Likely to Commit Suicide."

CHAPTER 4: CLIMBING THROUGH THE RANKS

1. "The Future of Women in Policing: Mandates for Action," International Association of Chiefs of Police bulletin, November 1998, 10; "Equality Denied: The Status of Women in Policing," National Center for Women & Policing bulletin, 2002, 7.

2. Deborah Parsons and Paul Jesilow, *In the Same Voice: Women and Men in Law Enforcement* (Santa Ana, CA: Seven Locks Press, 2001), 115–116.

3. Connie Fletcher, *Breaking and Entering: Women Cops Talk about Life in the Ultimate Men's Club* (New York: HarperCollins, 1995), 206.

4. Sandra K. Wells, "Women in Policing: The Experience of Female Police Chiefs and Deputy Police Chiefs" (PhD diss., Colorado State University, 2001), 76.

5. Ibid., 75.

6. Master Officer, Colorado Police Department, questionnaire, September 23, 2004 (see Appendix 2).

7. Police Officer II, Missouri, questionnaire, September 2004 (see Appendix 2).

8. Wells, "Women in Policing," 76.

9. Donna Leinwand, "Lawsuits of '70s Shape Current Police Leadership," *USA Today*, http://usatoday.printthis.clickability.com/pt/cpt?action=cpt&title=USATODAY.com+-+L (accessed September 9, 2004).

10. Penny Harrington and Kimberly A. Lonsway, "Current Barriers and Future Promise for Women in Policing," in *The Criminal Justice System and Women: Offenders, Prisoners, Victims, and Workers*, 3rd ed., edited by Barbara Raffel Price and Natalie J. Sokoloff (Boston: McGraw-Hill, 2004), 502.

11. Sergeant Lisa Grosskrueger, Arapahoe County, Colorado, Sheriff's Department, questionnaire, September 23, 2004 (see Appendix 2).

12. Jennifer Brown and Frances Heidensohn, *Gender and Policing: Comparative Perspectives* (New York: St. Martin's Press, 2000), 141.

13. Leinwand, "Lawsuits of the '70s."
14. Wells, "Women in Policing," 74.
15. Ibid.
16. Wells, "Women in Policing," 106.
17. Ibid.
18. Brown and Heidensohn, *Gender and Policing*, 146.
19. Wells, "Women in Policing," 117.
20. Brown and Heidensohn, *Gender and Policing*, 146.
21. Wells, "Women in Policing," 117–118.
22. Ibid., 119.
23. Marion E. Gold, *Top Cops: Profiles of Women in Command* (Chicago: Brittany, 1999), 105–107.
24. Grosskrueger, questionnaire.
25. Officer Jean Marie Bready, questionnaire, May 4, 2004 (see Appendix 1).
26. Officer Kristin Touchstone, questionnaire, June 2, 2004 (see Appendix 1).
27. Lieutenant Barbara Steinberg, questionnaire, May 18, 2004 (see Appendix 1).
28. Lieutenant, Arizona Police Department, questionnaire, September 23, 2004 (see Appendix 2).
29. Patrol Officer Suzette Freidenberger, Grand Junction, Colorado, Police Department, questionnaire, September 24, 2004 (see Appendix 2).
30. Wells, "Women in Policing," 58.
31. Lieutenant Deborah J. Cady, questionnaire, September 23, 2004 (see Appendix 2).

CHAPTER 5: REACHING THE PINNACLE

1. Sandra K. Wells, "Women in Policing: The Experience of Female Police Chiefs and Deputy Police Chiefs" (PhD diss., Colorado State University, 2001), 83.
2. Sean A. Grennan, "The Past, Present, and Future of Women in Policing," in *It's a Crime: Women and Justice*, 2nd ed., edited by Roslyn Muraskin (Upper Saddle River, NJ: Prentice Hall, 2000), 387–391.
3. "Number of Women in Policing Decreasing: Enormous Gender Gap Found in Rate of Police Brutality," Feminist Majority Foundation, April 30, 2002, http://www.feminist.org/news/presstory.asp?id=6499 (accessed May 3, 2004).
4. Ibid.
5. Grennan, "Past, Present and Future," 396.

6. B. R. Price and S. Gavin, "A Century of Women in Policing," in *Modern Police Administration*, edited by D. O. Schultz (Houston, TX: Gulf Publishing, 1981), 109–122.

7. Wells, "Women in Policing," 121.

8. Ibid., 120.

9. Jennifer Brown and Frances Heidensohn, *Gender and Policing: Comparative Perspectives* (New York: St. Martin's Press, 2000), 147.

10. Officer Jean Marie Bready, questionnaire, May 4, 2004 (see Appendix 1).

11. Chief Lynne Johnson, questionnaire, February 10, 2005 (see Appendix 1).

12. Wells, "Women in Policing," 123.

13. Ibid., 128.

14. Ibid.

15. Deborah Parsons and Paul Jesilow, *In the Same Voice: Women and Men in Law Enforcement* (Santa Ana, CA: Seven Locks Press, 2001), 118–120.

16. Connie Fletcher, *Breaking and Entering: Women Cops Talk about Life in the Ultimate Men's Club* (New York: HarperCollins, 1995), 283, 297.

17. Lisa Rein, "Woman Is Acting Chief in Fairfax; Police Veteran to Seek Permanent Position," *Washington Post*, January 27, 2004, B1.

18. Ibid.

19. Hawaii Joint Police Association, First Annual Salute to Women, Aiea, Hawaii, May 7, 1999.

20. Marion E. Gold, *Top Cops: Profiles of Women in Command* (Chicago: Brittany, 1999), 105–115.

21. Penny Harrington and Kimberly A. Lonsway, "Current Barriers and Future Promise for Women in Policing," in *The Criminal Justice System and Women: Offenders, Prisoners, Victims, and Workers*, 3rd ed., edited by Barbara Raffel Price and Natalie J. Sokoloff (Boston: McGraw-Hill, 2004), 503.

22. Tataboline Brant, "Trooper Director Proud of Her Troops," *Anchorage Daily News*, February 1, 2004, http://www.adn.com/alaska/story/4694326P-4645722c.html (accessed September 8, 2004).

23. Wells, "Women in Policing," 81.

24. Ibid.

25. Ibid.

26. Ibid., 82–83.

27. Ibid., 80.

28. Ibid.

29. Ibid., 83–85.

30. Ibid., 83.

31. Roslyn Muraskin and Albert R. Roberts, *It's a Crime: Women and Justice*, 2nd ed. (Upper Saddle River, NJ: Prentice Hall, 2000).

32. Ibid., 393.

33. Wells, "Women in Policing," 126.

34. Ibid., 125–126.

35. Ibid., 125.

36. "San Francisco Taps Female Police Chief," http://abclocal.go.com/kabc/news/041204_nw_sf_police_chief.html (accessed August 29, 2004).

37. Bill D'Agostino, "City to Hire First Female Police Chief," *Palo Alto Weekly*, February 7, 2003, http://www.paloaltoonline.com/weekly/morgue/2003/2003_02_07.qchief07mb.html (accessed August 29, 2004).

38. Brant, "Trooper Director Proud of Her Troops."

CHAPTER 6: ADVANTAGES WOMEN BRING TO LAW ENFORCEMENT

1. M. J. Palmiotto, "The Influence of Community in Community Policing in the Twenty-First Century," in *Visions for Change*, 2nd ed., edited by Roslyn Muraskin and Albert R. Roberts (Upper Saddle River, NJ: Prentice Hall, 1999), 133–137.

2. Muriel J. Whetstone, "Atlanta's Top Cop (Police Chief Beverly J. Harvard)," *Ebony*, March 1, 1995, http://www.highbeam.com/library/doc3.asp?ctrlInfo+Round7%3AProd%ADOC%3APri (accessed September 15, 2004).

3. Barbara Gordon, "Devlin Named Acting Chief," *Fairfax Chronicle*, March 3, 2004, http://www.chroniclenewspapers.com/articles/2004/03/03/news/news04.txt (accessed September 15, 2004).

4. Penny Harrington, "Hiring and Retaining More Women: The Advantages to Law Enforcement Agencies," Spring 2003, http://www.pennyharrington.com/hireandretain.htm.

5. Penny Harrington and Kimberly A. Lonsway, "Current Barriers and Future Promise for Women in Policing," in *The Criminal Justice System and Women: Offenders, Prisoners, Victims, and Workers*, edited by Barbara Raffel Price and Natalie J. Sokoloff (Boston: McGraw-Hill, 2004), 496.

6. Kimberly A. Lonsway, Michelle Wood, and Katherine Spillar, "Officer, Gender and Excessive Force," *Law and Order* (December 2002): 60–66; "Number of Women in Policing Decreasing; Enormous Gender Gap Found in Rate of Police Brutality," Feminist Majority Foundation, April 30, 2002, http://www.womenandpolicing.org/article.asp?id=6499 (accessed May 3, 2004).

7. Sandra K. Wells, "Women in Policing: The Experience of Female Police Chiefs and Deputy Police Chiefs" (PhD diss., Colorado State University, 2001), 59.

8. Katherine Spillar and Penny Harrington, "This Is What You Get When Men Rule Roost," *Los Angeles Times*, February 18, 2000, http://www.womenandpolicing.org/oped021800.asp (accessed March 8, 2004).

9. Frank Schmalleger, *Criminology Today: An Integrative Introduction*, 3rd ed. (Upper Saddle River, NJ: Prentice Hall, 2002), 275.

10. Wells, "Women in Policing," 93.

11. David Holmstrom, "Women Officers Arrest the Gender Gap," *Christian Science Monitor*, January 12, 2000, 11, http://web7.epnet.com/citation.asp?tb=1&_ut=dbs+aph+sid+567762D6%2D8458%2D43D (accessed April 1, 2004).

12. Kimberly Lonsway, "Tearing Down the Wall: Problems with Consistency, Validity, and Adverse Impact of Physical Agility Testing in Police Selection," *Police Quarterly* 6, no. 3 (September 2003): 3.

13. Penny Harrington et al., "Men, Women, and Police Excessive Force: A Tale of Two Genders," April 2002, http://www.pennyharrington.com/excessiveforceanaly.htm (accessed April 9, 2004).

14. "Number of Women in Policing Decreasing."

15. Lonsway, Wood, and Spillar, "Officer, Gender and Excessive Force," 496.

16. Zev Yaroslavsky and Katherine Spillar, "More Women in the Ranks Would Stem LAPD Brutality," *Los Angeles Times*, October 2, 2000, http://www.womenandpolicing.org/oped100200.asp (accessed May 3, 2004).

17. Harrington et al., "Men, Women and Police Excessive Force."

18. Edwin J. Delattre, *Character and Cops: Ethics in Policing* (Washington, DC: AEI Press, 1996), 12.

19. R. J. Homant and D. B. Kennedy, "Police Perceptions of Spouse Abuse—A Comparison of Male and Female Officers," *Journal of Criminal Justice* 13 (1985): 29–47.

20. Penny Harrington, "Hiring and Retaining More Women: The Advantages to Law Enforcement Agencies," National Center for Women & Policing, Spring 2003 (citing article "The Victims' View: Domestic Violence and Police Response," August 2003), http://www.pennyharrington.com/hireandretain.htm (accessed May 25, 2004).

21. "Recruiting and Retaining Women: A Self-Assessment Guide for Law Enforcement," National Center for Women & Policing bulletin, n.d., 25.

22. Jennifer Weil, "Women Police Are on the Beat, but Not on the Force," *Journal News*, May 7, 2004, http://www.thejournalnews.com/weekly/050704/a0lit0507femalec.html (accessed September 9, 2004).

23. Deborah Parsons and Paul Jesilow, *In the Same Voice: Women and Men in Law Enforcement* (Santa Ana, CA: Seven Locks Press, 2001), 147.

24. Susan L. Miller, "Arrest Policies for Domestic Violence and Their Implications for Battered Women," in *The Criminal Justice System and Women: Offenders, Victims, and Workers*, 2nd ed., edited by Barbara Raffel Price and Natalie J. Sokoloff (New York: McGraw-Hill, 1995), 294–295.

25. Susan Ehrlich Martin, *Breaking and Entering: Police Women on Patrol* (Berkeley, CA: University of California Press, 1980), 38; Peter Horne, *Women in Law Enforcement*, 2nd ed. (Springfield, IL: Charles C. Thomas, 1980), 86–87.

26. Weil, "Women Police Are on the Beat."

27. A. Eagly and B. Johnson, "Gender and the Emergence of Leaders: A Meta-Analysis," *Psychological Bulletin* 108 (1990): 233–256.

28. Peter G. Northouse, *Leadership: Theory and Practice*, 2nd ed. (Thousand Oaks, CA: Sage, 2001), 55.

29. Wells, "Women in Policing," 99.

30. Northouse, *Leadership*, 55–56.

31. Sarah Karush, "After Breaking Gender Barrier, Detroit's New Top Cop Sets Out to Fix Ailing System," *Detroit News*, November 8, 2003, http://www.detnews.com/2003/metro/0311/10metro-319356.htm (accessed September 9, 2004).

32. Whetstone, "Atlanta's Top Cop."

33. Lieutenant Barbara Steinberg, questionnaire, May 18, 2004 (see Appendix 1).

34. Noel C. Paul, "The Woman Chosen to Lead Boston's Police," *Christian Science Monitor*, March 16, 2004, http://www.csmonitor.com/2004/0316/p02s01-usju.htm (accessed September 15, 2004).

35. Chief Lynne Johnson, questionnaire, September 2004 (see Appendix 1).

36. Jim Herron Zamora and Cicero Estrella, "A Low-Profile Chief Heather Fong May Serve Behind the Scenes, but She's Tough and Reform Minded," *San Francisco Chronicle*, May 2, 2004, http://www.sfgate.com/cgi-bin/article.cgi?file=/c/a/2004/05/02FONG.TMP7type=printa (accessed September 15, 2004).

CHAPTER 7: TO BE A SUCCESSFUL POLICE WOMAN

1. "Number of Women in Policing Decreasing: Enormous Gender Gap Found in Rate of Police Brutality," Feminist Majority Foundation, April 30, 2002, http://www.feminist.org/news/presstory.asp?id=6499 (accessed May 3, 2004).

2. Louis M. Harris and J. Norman Baldwin, "Voluntary Turnover of

Field Operations Officers: A Test of Confluency Theory," *Journal of Criminal Justice* 27, no. 6 (1999): 485.

3. Ibid.

4. "The Future of Women in Policing: Mandates for Action" (N.p.: International Association of Chiefs of Police, 1998), 9.

5. Sandra K. Wells, "Women in Policing: The Experience of Female Police Chiefs and Deputy Police Chiefs" (PhD diss., Colorado State University, 2001), 102–103.

6. Ibid., 102.

7. Ibid., 105.

8. Detective Mianna Sorenson, questionnaire, September 23, 2004 (see Appendix 2).

9. Penny Harrington, "Advice to Women Beginning a Career in Policing," *Women and Criminal Justice* 14, no. 1 (2002): 10–11.

10. Wells, "Women in Policing," 108.

11. Ibid., 109.

12. Edwin J. Delattre, *Character and Cops: Ethics in Policing*, 3rd ed. (Washington, DC: AEI Press, 1996), 33.

13. Detective Lisa Grosskrueger, questionnaire, September 23, 2004 (see Appendix 2).

Bibliography

Aamodt, Michael G., and Nicole A. Stalnaker. "Police Officer Suicide: Frequency and Officer Profiles." http://www.radford.edu/~maamodt/PoliceResearch/PoliceSuicide.pdf (accessed August 29, 2004).

Abelson, Jenn. "Gender Bias Cited by Ex-Major." *Boston Globe*, June 23, 2003, B1. http://nl.newsbank.com/nl-search/we/Archives?p_action=print (accessed May 31, 2004).

———. "Trooper Files Sex-Bias Claim." *Boston Globe*, January 20, 2004, B1. http://nl.newsbank.com/nl-search/we/Archives?p_action=print (accessed May 31, 2004).

Adler, S. J. "Suits over Sexual Harassment Prove Difficult Due to Issue of Definition." *Wall Street Journal*, October 9, 1991.

Armstrong, Michael. "Homer Woman Graduates from Public Safety Academy." *Homer News*, June 10, 2004. http://homernews.com/stories/061004/new_061004new014001.shtml (accessed September 8, 2004).

Austin, Thomas L., and Don Hummer. "What Do College Students Think of Policewomen? An Attitudinal Assessment of Future Law Enforcement Personnel." *Women and Criminal Justice* 10, no. 4 (1999): 1–24.

Balkin, Joseph. "Why Policemen Don't Like Policewomen." *Journal of Police Science and Administration* 16, no. 1 (1988): 29–37.

Barker, Joan C. *Danger, Duty, and Disillusion: The Worldview of Los Angeles Police Officers*. Prospect Heights, NJ: Waveland Press, 1999.

Bartol, C. R., G. T. Bergen, Volckens J. Seager, and K. M. Knoras. "Women in Small-Town Policing." *Criminal Justice and Behavior* (September 1, 1992): 240–259.

Bell, D. J. "Policewomen: Myths and Reality." *Journal of Police Science and Administration* 10 (1982): 112–120.

Belnap, J., and J. K. Shelly. "The New Lone Ranger: Policewomen on Patrol." *American Journal of Police* (December 1992): 47–75.

Berg, B. L., and K. J. Budnick. "Defeminization of Women in Law Enforcement: A New Twist in the Traditional Police Personality." *Journal of Police Science and Administration* 14 (1986): 314–319.

Brant, Tataboline. "Trooper Director Proud of Her Troops." *Anchorage Daily News*, February 1, 2004. http://www.adn.com/alaska/story/4694326p-4645722c.html (accessed September 8, 2004).

Brown, Jennifer, and Frances Heidensohn. *Gender and Policing: Comparative Perspectives*. New York: St. Martin's Press, 2000.

Bruce, Leona. "The Handbook of Texas Online." http://www.tsha.utexas.edu/handbook/online/articles/view/BB/fbacq.html (accessed April 2, 2004).

Buhrke, Robin A. *A Matter of Justice: Lesbians and Gay Men in Law Enforcement*. New York: Routledge, 1996.

Burns, S. E. "Issues in Workplace Sexual Harassment Law and Related Social Science Research." *Author's Abstract Journal of Social Science*, no. 51 (1995): 191–198.

Buwalda, Imra Wann. "The Policewoman—Yesterday, Today and Tomorrow." *Journal of Social Hygiene* 31, no. 5 (May 1945).

California Highway Patrol. "From Secretary to Safeguarding the Public: Assistant Chief Bonnie Stanton." http://www.chp.ca.gov/recruting/html/bonnie_stanton.html (accessed September 17, 2004).

Constant, Terry. "Not So Obvious Police Stress." http://www.tearsofacop/com/police/articles/constant.html (accessed August 17, 2004).

Cramer, Maria. "Female Officer Files Harassment Lawsuit." *Boston Globe*, March 28, 2004, 1. http://nl.newsbank.com/nl-search/we/Archives?p_action=print (accessed March 31, 2004).

D'Agostino, Bill. "City to Hire First Female Police Chief." *Palo Alto Weekly*, February 7, 2003. http://www.paloaltoonline.com/weekly.morgue/2003/2003_02_07.qchief007mb.html (accessed August 29, 2004).

Daum, J. M., and C. M. Johns. "Police Work from a Woman's Perspective." *Police Chief*, September 1994.

Delattre, Edwin J. *Character and Cops: Ethics in Policing*. Washington, DC: AEI Press, 1996.

Denver Public Safety Recruitment. "Denver Police Department Employee Groups." http://www.denvergov.org/Recruit/template113569.asp (accessed August 17, 2004).

"Detroit Chief of Police." http://www.ci.detroit.mi.us/police/dept/chief/cop.htm (accessed September 9, 2004).

Detzer, Karl. "Detroit's Lady Cops." *American Mercury*, March 1942.

Eagly, A., and B. Johnson. "Gender and the Emergency of Leaders: A Meta-analysis." *Psychological Bulletin* 108 (1990): 233–256.

Edler, Molly Snyder. "Milwaukee Talks: Nan Hegerty." Milwaukee.com, March 9, 2004. http://www.onmilwaukee.com/articles/print/hegertytalks.html (accessed September 15, 2004).

"Equality Denied: The Status of Women and Policing: 2001." National Center for Women & Policing bulletin, April 2002.

"Evaluation of the Impact of Affirmative Action Policies on Women in Law Enforcement." http://www.geocities.com/CapitolHill/8512/eval.html (accessed May 3, 2004).

Feinman, C. *Women in the Criminal Justice System*. 2nd ed. New York: Praeger, 1986.

"Female Police Officer Reinstated after Three-Year Sexual Harassment Battle." *Women & Policing News Wire*, July 25, 2002. http://www.womenandpolicing.org/article.asp?id=6729 (accessed March 8, 2004).

"Female Police Psychology." http://www.angelfire.com/vt/policepsychology/page5.html (accessed August 29, 2004).

Feminist Majority Foundation. "First Ever National Police Leadership Conference for Women Calls for Gender-Balance in Law Enforcement." http://www.feminist.org/news/pr/pr111395.html (accessed June 2, 1999).

"Fire When Ready, Ma'am." *Time*, January 15, 1990.

"First Women Sheriffs in the United States of America." http://www.geocities.com/vbenson_2000/sheriffs.htm (accessed April 2, 2004).

Flanders, C. *Breakthrough the Career: Woman's Guide to Shattering the Glass Ceiling*. London: Paul Chapman, 1994.

Fletcher, Connie. *Breaking and Entering: Women Cops Talk about Life in the Ultimate Men's Club*. New York: HarperCollins, 1995.

Fuoco, M. A. "City Force No. 1 in Women in Blue." *Pittsburgh Post-Gazette*, May 28, 1998.

"The Future of Women in Policing: Mandates for Action." International Association of Chiefs of Police bulletin, November 1998.

Garcia, Venessa. " 'Difference' in the Police Department: Women, Policing, and 'Doing Gender.' " *Journal of Contemporary Criminal Justice* 19, no. 3 (August 2003): 330–344.

Gay Officers Action League (GOAL). http://www.goalny.org/mission.htm (accessed August 17, 2004).

Gay Police Officers Action League of DC. http://www.goaldc.com/ (accessed August 17, 2004).

Georgia Sheriffs' Association. http://www.georgiasheriffs.org/ (accessed April 2, 2004).

Gerber, Gwendolyn L. *Women and Men Police Officers: Status, Gender, and Personality*. Westport, CT: Praeger, 2001.

Gilmartin, Kevin M. *Emotional Survival for Law Enforcement: A Guide for Officers and Their Families*. Tucson, AZ: E-S Press, 2002.

Gold, Marion E. *Top Cops: Profiles of Women in Command*. Chicago: Brittany, 1999.

Goldfarb, Dan. "The Effects of Stress on Police Officers." http://www.heavybadge.com/efstress.htm (accessed August 17, 2004).

Gordon, Barbara. "Devlin Named Acting Chief." *Fairfax Chronicle*, March 3, 2004. http://www.chroniclenewspapers.com/articles/2004/03/03/news/news04.txt (accessed September 15, 2004).

Gossett, Jennifer Lynn, and Joyce E. Williams. "Perceived Discrimination among Women in Law Enforcement." *Women & Criminal Justice* 10 (1998): 53–73.

Grennan, Sean A. "The Past, Present, and Future of Women in Policing." In *It's a Crime: Women and Justice*. 2nd ed., edited by Roslyn Muraskin. Upper Saddle River, NJ: Prentice Hall, 2000.

Hale, Donna C., and Mark Lanier. "The Next Generation: Women in Policing in the Twenty-First Century." In *Visions for Change: Crime and Justice in the Twenty-First Century*. 2nd ed., edited by Roslyn Muraskin and Albert R. Roberts. Upper Saddle River, NJ: Prentice Hall, 1999.

Hamilton, Mary E. "Woman's Place in the Police Department." *American City* 32 (February 1925).

Hansen, Bob. "Lady Sheriff an Unofficial Official." *The Hawk Eye*, July 23, 2000. http://www.thehawkeye.com/columns.Hansen/2000/cha72300.html (accessed April 2, 2004).

Harrington, Penny. "Hiring and Retaining More Women: The Advantages to Law Enforcement Agencies." Spring 2003. http://www.pennyharrington.com/hireandretain.htm (accessed April 9, 2004).

———. "Men, Women, and Police Excessive Force: A Tale of Two Genders." April 2002. http://www.pennyharrington.com/excessiveforceanaly.htm (accessed April 9, 2004).

———. *Triumph of Spirit*. Chicago: Brittany Publications, 1999.

Harrington, Penny, and Kimberly A. Lonsway. "Current Barriers and Future Promise for Women in Policing." In *The Criminal Justice System and Women*. 3rd ed., edited by Barbara Raffel Price and Natalie J. Sokoloff. Boston: McGraw-Hill, 2004.

Harris, Louis M., and J. Norman Baldwin. "Voluntary Turnover of Field Operations Officers: A Test of Confluency Theory." *Journal of Criminal Justice* 27, no. 6 (1999): 483–493.

Hawaii Joint Police Association. First Annual Salute to Women. May 7, 1999.

———. Second Annual Salute to Women. May 5, 2000.

Heidensohn, F. *Women in Control? The Role of Women in Law Enforcement*. Oxford: Clarendon Press, 1992.

Heim, Pat. *Hardball for Women*. New York: Plume, 1992.

Heim, Pat, and Susan K. Golant. *Smashing the Glass Ceiling*. New York: Simon and Schuster, 1995.

Helgesen, Sally. *The Female Advantage: Women's Ways of Leadership*. New York: Doubleday, 1990.

"Hiring and Retaining More Women: The Advantages to Law Enforcement Agencies." National Center for Women & Policing bulletin, Spring 2003. http://www.pennyharrington.com/hireandretain.htm (accessed May 25, 2004).

Holm, Jeanne. *Women in the Military: An Unfinished Revolution*. Novato, CA: Presidio Press, 1982.

Holstrom, David. "Women Officers Arrest the Gender Gap." *Christian Science Monitor*, January 12, 2000, 11. http://web7.epnet.com/citation.asp?tb=1&_ut=dbs+aph+sid+56776D6%2D8458%2D43D (accessed April 1, 2004).

Homant, R. J., and D. B. Kennedy. "Police Perceptions of Spouse Abuse—A Comparison of Male and Female Officers." *Journal of Criminal Justice* 13 (1985): 9–47.

Horne, Peter. *Women in Law Enforcement*. 2nd ed. Springfield, IL: Charles C. Thomas, 1980.

Hughes, Michael, and Carolyn J. Kroehler. *Sociology: The Core*. 7th ed. Boston: McGraw-Hill, 2005.

"Important Firsts in Women's Law Enforcement." http://www.geocities.com/vbenson_2000/firsts.htm (accessed May 3, 2004).

Ionia County. "History of the Ionia County [Michigan] Office of Sheriff." http://www.ioniacounty.org/sheriff/Sheriff_history.asp (accessed April 2, 2004).

"Jury Awards over $3 Million to Women Police Officers in Gender Bias Case." *Women & Policing News Wire*, May 13, 2002. http://www.womenandpolicing.org/article.asp?id=6525 (accessed March 8, 2004).

Karush, Sarah. "After Breaking Gender Barrier, Detroit's New Top Cop Sets Out to Fix Ailing System." *Detroit News*, November 8, 2003. http://www.detnews.com/2003/metro/0311/10/metro-f319356.htm (accessed September 9, 2004).

Kinnon, Joy Bennett. "Top Black Cops: African-American Chiefs Take the Helm in Metropolitan America." http://www.findarticles.com/p/articles/mi_m1077/is_n12/v53?ai_21225417/print (accessed September 9, 2004).

Lamanna, Mary Ann, and Agnes Riedmann. *Marriages and Families: Making Choices and Facing Change*. 5th ed. Belmont, CA: Wadsworth, 1994.

"LAPD Announces New Initiative to Increase Women Officers." *Women & Policing News Wire*, December 17, 2002 (accessed March 8, 2004).

Lauer, Robert H. *Social Problems and the Quality of Life*. 6th ed. Madison, WI: Brown and Benchmark, 1995.

Leinwand, Donna. "Lawsuits of '70s Shape Current Police Leadership." *USA Today*. http://usatoday.printthis.clickability.com/pt/cpt?action=cpt&title=USATODAY.com+-+L (accessed September 9, 2004).

Lieberman, J. "The Effects of Sex Bias in the Evaluation of Police Reports, 1989." Manuscript.

Lonsway, Kimberly. "Tearing Down the Wall: Problems with Consistency, Validity, and Adverse Impact of Physical Agility Testing in Police Selection." *Police Quarterly* 6, no. 3 (September 2003): 237–277.

Lonsway, Kimberly A., Michelle Wood, and Katherine Spillar. "Officer, Gender and Excessive Force." *Law and Order*, December 2002, 60–66.

Los Angeles Police Department. "Civil Rights Consent Decree Overview." http://www.lapdonline.org/inside_lapd/cd/consent_decree.htm (accessed May 3, 2004).

"MA Women Officers File Sex Discrimination Suit." *Women & Policing News Wire*, November 7, 2002. http://www.womenandpolicing.org/article.asp?idd=7259 (accessed March 8, 2004).

Martin, Susan Ehrlich. *Breaking and Entering: Police Women on Patrol*. Berkeley: University of California Press, 1980.

———. "Female Officers on the Move? A Status Report on Women in Policing." In *Critical Issues in Policing: Contemporary Readings*, edited by R. Dunham and G. Alpert. Prospect Heights, IL: Waveland Press, 1989.

———. "The Interactive Effects of Race and Sex on Women Police Officers." In *The Criminal Justice System and Women: Offenders, Prisoners, Victims, and Workers*. 3rd ed., edited by Barbara Raffel Price and Natalie J. Sokoloff. New York: McGraw-Hill, 2004.

Martin, Susan Ehrlich, and Nancy C. Jurik. *Doing Justice, Doing Gender: Women in Law and Criminal Justice Occupations*. Thousand Oaks, CA: Sage Publications, 1996.

McPherson, James M. *Battle Cry of Freedom, The Civil War Era*. New York: Ballantine Books, 1988.

Meccouri, Linda L. "'Making It': Resilient Women Overcoming Adversity in Defiance of Negative Predictors of Success." Diss., University of New Mexico, December 1995.

Meers, Erik. "Good Cop Gay Cop: From the Beat Patrol to the Precinct House, Gay and Lesbian Police Officers are Shattering the Blue Wall of Silence." *Advocate*, March 3, 1998. http://www.findarticles.com/p/articles/mi_m1589/is-n754ai_20350566 (accessed August 17, 2004).

Merko, Alida V., Kate Bagley, and Michele C. Bafuma. "In Defense of Affirmative Action for Women in the Criminal Justice Profession." In *It's a Crime: Women and Justice*. 2nd ed., edited by Roslyn Muraskin. Upper Saddle River, NJ: Prentice Hall, 2000.

Milgram, Donna. "Recruiting Women to Policing: Practical Strategies That Work." *Police Chief*, April 2002. http://www.jwitts.com/html/the_police_chief_magazine__rec.html (accessed May 25, 2004).

Miller, Susan L. "Arrest Policies for Domestic Violence and Their Implications for Battered Women." In *The Criminal Justice System and Women: Offenders, Victims, and Workers*. 2nd ed., edited by Barbara Raffel Price and Natalie J. Sokoloff. New York: McGraw-Hill, 1995.

Miller, Susan L., Kay B. Forest, and Nancy C. Jurik. "Lesbians in Policing: Perceptions and Work Experiences with the Macho Cop Culture." In *The Criminal Justice System and Women: Offenders, Prisoners, Victims, and Workers,* 3rd ed., edited by Barbara Raffel Price and Natalie J. Sokoloff. Boston: McGraw-Hill, 2004.

Mitchell, Brian. *Weak Link: The Feminization of the American Military*. Washington, DC: Regnery Gateway, 1989.

"More Women Police File Sex Discrimination Suits." *Women & Policing News Wire,* August 19, 1999. http://www.womenandpolicing.org/article.asp?id=398 (accessed March 8, 2004).

Moyer, Imogene L. *The Changing Roles of Women in the Criminal Justice System*. 2nd ed. Prospect Heights, IL: Waveland Press, 1992.

Munger, Elizabeth. "Policewomen for Smaller Cities." *The Woman Citizen* 10, no. 4 (July 11, 1925).

Muraskin, Roslyn. *It's a Crime: Women and Justice*. 2nd ed. Upper Saddle River, NJ: Prentice Hall, 2000.

Muraskin, Roslyn, and Albert R. Roberts. *Visions for Change: Crime and Justice in the Twenty-first Century*. 2nd ed. Upper Saddle River, NJ: Prentice Hall, 1999.

Myers, Gloria E. *A Municipal Mother: Portland's Lola Greene Baldwin, America's First Policewoman*. Corvallis: Oregon State University Press, 1995.

Nichols, Nancy A., ed. *Reach for the Top*. Boston: Harvard Business School Press, 1994.

Northouse, Peter G. *Leadership Theory and Practice*. 2nd ed. Thousand Oaks, CA: Sage Publications, 2001.

"Number of Women in Policing Decreasing: Enormous Gender Gap Found in Rate of Police Brutality." National Center for Women & Policing. http:///www.womenandpolicing.org/article.asp?id=6499 (accessed May 5, 2004).

"NYC Police Less Likely to Commit Suicide Than NYC Citizens, New York Weill Cornell Study Shows." http://www.med.cornell.edu/news/press/2002/12_19_02_b.html (accessed August 29, 2004).

O'Gorman, Patricia. *Dancing Backwards in High Heels: How Women Master the Art of Resilience*. City Center, MN: Hazelden Educational Materials, 1994.

"$1 Million Awarded to MA State Troopers in Pregnancy Discrimination Case." *Women & Policing News Wire*, October 8, 2002. http://www.womenandpolicing.org/article.asp?id=7058 (accessed March 8, 2004).

O'Shaughnessy, Lynn. "Police Academy Training Has Changed to Accommodate Women." *Memphis Press-Scimitar*, 1980. http://www.memphispolice.org?Women%20%20In%20the%20News (accessed May 25, 2004).

———. "'Weaker Sex': Police Cadets Put Cloud on Training Program." *Memphis Press-Scimitar*, 1980. http://www.memphispolice.org/Women%20in%20Policing%20-%20In%20the%20News (accessed May 25, 2004).

Palmiotto, M. J. "The Influence of Community in Community Policing in the Twenty-first Century." In *It's a Crime: Women and Justice*, edited by Roslyn Muraskin and Albert R. Roberts. Upper Saddle River, NJ: Prentice Hall, 1999.

Parsons, Deborah, and Paul Jesilow. *In the Same Voice, Women and Men in Law Enforcement*. Santa Ana, CA: Seven Locks Press, 2001.

Paul, Noel C. "The Woman Chosen to Lead Boston's police." *Christian Science Monitor*, March 16, 2004. http://www.csmonitor.com/2004/0316/p02s01-usju.htm (accessed September 15, 2004).

Pearsall, Richard. "Burlco to Swear in First Female Sheriff." *Courier-Post*, January 1, 2002. http://www.southjerseynews.com/issues/january/m010102h.htm (accessed April 2, 2004).

"Pennsylvania Police Ignore Progressive Physical Testing Trends." *Women & Policing News Wire*, December 29, 2002. http://www.women andpolicing.org/article.asp?id=7371 (accessed March 8, 2004).

"Police Suicide, and Stress: Facts and Information." http://www.police stress.com/wsn3AAE.html (accessed August 29, 2004).

Polisar, Joseph, and Donna Milgram. "Recruiting, Integrating and Retaining Women Police Officers: Strategies That Work." October 1998. http://www.iwitts.com/html.the_police_chief_magazine__str.html (accessed May 25, 2004).

Pratt, Chuck. "Why Do Police Officers Have Such an Outlandish Rate of Marital and Domestic Failure and Calamity?" http://www.geocities.com/~halbrown/police_affairs.html (accessed August 17, 2004).

Price, B. R., and S. Gavin. "A Century of Women in Policing." In *Modern Police Administration*, edited by D. O. Schultz. Houston, TX: Gulf Publishing, 1981.

Price, Barbara Raffel, and Natalie J. Sokoloff, eds. *The Criminal Justice System and Women*. New York: McGraw-Hill, 1995.

———, eds. *The Criminal Justice System and Women*. 3rd ed. Boston: McGraw-Hill, 2004.

"Recruiting and Retaining Women: A Self-Assessment Guide for Law Enforcement." National Center for Women & Policing bulletin, n.d.

"Recruiting Women." *Police Chief*, April 2002.

Rein, Lisa. "Woman Is Acting Chief in Fairfax: Police Veteran to Seek Permanent Position." *Washington Post*, January 27, 2004, B1.

Rogers, Steven L. *21st Century Policing: Community Policing*. Fresh Meadows, NY: Looseleaf Law, 1998.

Rosener, Judy B. *America's Competitive Secret: Women Managers*. New York: Oxford University Press, 1994.

"San Francisco Taps Female Police Chief." KABC-TV, Los Angeles. http://abclocal.go.com/kabc/news/041204_nw_sf_police_chief.html (accessed August 29, 2004).

Schmallenger, Frank. *Criminology Today: An Integrative Introduction*. 3rd ed. Upper Saddle River, NJ: Prentice Hall, 2002.

Schulz, Dorothy Moses. "California Dreaming: Leading the Way to Gender-Free Police Management." *CJ The Americas* 7, no. 1 (1994): 8–10.

———. *From Social Worker to Crimefighter: Women in United States Municipal Policing*. Westport, CT: Praeger, 1995.

———. "Invisible No More: A Social History of Women in U. S. Policing." In *The Criminal Justice System and Women*. 3rd ed., edited by Barbara Raffel Price and Natalie J. Sokoloff. Boston: McGraw-Hill, 2004.

———. "The Police Matron Movement: Paving the Way for Policewomen." *Police Studies: The International Review of Police Development* 12 (1989): 115–124.

———. "Policewomen in the 1950s: Paving the Way for Patrol." *Women and Criminal Justice* (April 1993): 5–30.

"Sexual Harassment Allegations Believed to Have Caused Chief's Resignation." *Women & Policing News Wire*, August 16, 2002. http://www.womenandpolicing.org/article.asp?id=6797 (accessed March 8, 2004).

Shepherd, Jon M. *Sociology*. Belmont, CA: Wadsworth, 1999.

Siegel, Larry J. *Criminology*. 2nd ed. New York: West, 1985.

Silvestri, Marisa. *Women in Charge: Policing, Gender and Leadership*. Portland, OR: Willan, 2003.

Smith, Elizabeth Simpson. *Breakthrough: Women in Law Enforcement*. New York: Walker, 1982.

Spillar, Katherine, and Penny Harrington. "This Is What You Get When Men Rule Roost." *Los Angeles Times*, February 18, 2000. http://www.womenandpolicing.org/oped021800.asp (accessed March 8, 2004).

"Status of Women in Policing: 1998." Washington, DC: National Center for Women & Policing, 1998.

Steele, Jeanette. "Marines about to Get a First—General Mom." *Union-Tribune*, March 22, 2002.

Stephens, W. Richard. *Careers in Criminal Justice*. 2nd ed. Boston: Allyn and Bacon, 2002.

"Three Female Police Officers Win $2.5 Million Sex Harassment Suit." *Women & Policing News Wire*, June 6, 2003. http://www.womenandpolicing.org/article.asp?id=7839 (accessed March 8, 2004).

"Two WA Women Police Officers Sue Police Department for Discrimination." *Women & Policing News Wire*, August 16, 2002. http://www.womenandpolicing.org/article.asp?id=6796 (accessed March 8, 2004).

UK Home Office. "Gay and Lesbian and Sexuality Issues." http://www.homeoffice.gov.uk/crimpol/police/equality/sexualityissues.html (accessed August 17, 2004).

U.S. Department of Justice. Bureau of Statistics. http://www.ojp.usdoj.gov/bjs/pub/ascii/sd97.txt (accessed April 2, 2004).

U.S. Equal Employment Opportunity Commission. "Facts about Pregnancy Discrimination." http://www.eeoc.gov/facts/fs-preg.html (accessed March 25, 2004).

Van Wormer, Catherine Stuart, and Clemens Bartollas. *Women and the Criminal Justice System*. Boston: Allyn and Bacon, 2000.

Vega, M., and I. Silverman. "Female Police Officers as Viewed by Their Male Counterparts." *Police Science* (May 1982).

"Veteran Woman Police Officer Claims Gender Discrimination." *Women & Policing News Wire*, June 26, 2003 (citing both the Boston *Globe* and the Associated Press). http://www.womenandpolicing.org/article.asp?id=7885 (accessed March 8, 2004).

Vollmer, August. "Meet the Lady Cop." *The Survey*, March 15, 1930.

Washington Association of Sheriffs and Police Chief. "Assessment Centers." http://www.waspc.org/assessment.shtml (accessed September 9, 2004).

Weil, Jennifer. "Women Police Are on the Beat, but Not in Force." *The Item*, May 7, 2004. http://www.thejournalnews.com/weekly/050704/a0lit0507femalec.html (accessed September 9, 2004).

Wells, Sandra K. "Women in Policing: The Experience of Female Police Chiefs and Deputy Police Chiefs." PhD diss., Colorado State University, Spring 2001.

Wertsch, T. L. "Walking the Thin Blue Line: Policewomen and Tokenism Today." *Women and Criminal Justice* (September 1998).

Whetstone, Muriel L. "Atlanta's Top Cop [Police Chief Beverly J. Harvard]." *Ebony*, March 1, 1995. http://www.highbeam.com/library/doc3.asp?ctrlInfo=Round7%3AProd%3ADOC%3APri.

"The Woman Chosen to Lead Boston's Police." *Christian Science Monitor*, March 18, 2004. http://www.csmonitor.com/2004/0316/p02s01-usju.htm (accessed September 15, 2004).

Women in Uniform: Exploding the Myths; Exploring the Facts. Washington, DC: Women's Research and Education Institute, 1998.

"Women to Ride in Police Cruisers." *Memphis Press-Scimitar*, January 12, 1970. http://www.memphispolice.org/Women%20inPolicing%20-%IN%the20News (accessed May 23, 2004).

"Workplace Issues: Pregnancy Issues in Law Enforcement." National Center for Women & Policing. http://www.womenandpolicing.org/workplace4~pregnancy.asp (accessed May 25, 2004).

"Workplace Issues: Recognizing Workplace Discrimination." National Center for Women & Policing. http://www.womenandpolicing.org/workplace2~harrassment.asp (accessed March 25, 2004).

Yaroslavsly, Zev, and Katherine Spillar. "More Women in the Ranks Would Stem LAPD Brutality." *Los Angeles Times*, October 2, 2002. http://www.womenandpolicing.org/oped100200.asp (accessed May 3, 2004).

Zamora, Jim Herron, and Cicero Estrella. "A Low-Profile Chief Heather Fong May Serve Behind the Scenes, but She's Tough and Reform Minded." *San Francisco Chronicle*, May 2, 2004. http://www.sfgate.com/cgi-bin/article.cgi?file=/c//a/2004/05/02FONG.TMP7type=printa (accessed September 15, 2004).

Index

About the Authors

SANDRA K. WELLS After 29 years, retired as Chief Investigator with the District Attorney's office in Pueblo, Colorado, and now teaches at Pueblo Community College and Colorado State University-Pueblo. She is the co-author of *Wicked Women* (2000) and *Fleecing Grandma and Grandpa* (Praeger, 2004).

BETTY L. ALT is Lecturer at Colorado State University and has published several books, including *Wicked Women* (2000), *Black Soldiers, White Wars* (Praeger, 2002), and *Fleecing Grandma and Grandpa* (Praeger, 2004).